Welcome to My
CLASSROOM

SECOND EDITION

Rob Jenkins

Cover image © Shutterstock, Inc.

Kendall Hunt
publishing company

www.kendallhunt.com
Send all inquiries to:
4050 Westmark Drive
Dubuque, IA 52004-1840

Copyright © 2016, 2018 by Rob Jenkins

ISBN 978-1-5249-5534-2

Printed in the United States of America

Contents

Part III: Essays on Thinking and Writing   147

Part IV: Essays on Issues in Higher Education   217

Part I

Essays on Classroom Management

1

Welcome to My Classroom

Good morning, everybody. My name is Rob Jenkins, and I'll be your instructor this semester. You can call me Mr. Jenkins or Professor Jenkins, for now. After you get your first essay back, you might want to call me something else.

Just kidding. I'm sure you'll do fine. I can promise you this: If you put as much effort into taking this class as I put into teaching it, you'll definitely learn something. Whether or not that effort translates into the grade you want remains to be seen. But we'll talk more about that later.

Believe it or not, I've been teaching this course for over thirty years. If you have no trouble believing that, please keep it to yourself. When I started teaching, in 1985, students did all their written work by hand. No one had an email address. Cell phones were the size of psychology textbooks and cost almost as much. Of course, as technology has advanced, I have too. So please, no handwritten essays. And no giant cell phones.

Over the years I've also learned a lot from my students, which has occasionally led me to change the way I do things. That's right, I learn from you. Students are always guinea pigs, whether they realize it or not. But you can rest easy, knowing I've already made most of my mistakes on the thousands of students who preceded you.

Probably.

On the other hand, I do still use a lot of the same activities and assignments I used twenty years ago, because they work. Besides, why waste a perfectly good set of mimeographed notes when the ink is still readable? Anybody know what a mimeograph machine is? Never mind.

Anyway, enough about me. Let's talk about you. The first thing you need to understand is that, as far as I'm concerned, you're all adults. Of course, some of you are literally adults, with jobs, families, and mortgages that are now worth more than your house—just like me. But even if you're a seventeen-year-old dual-enrollment student, while you're in my class you're an adult, and I intend to treat you as such.

At the same time, I expect you to act like adults. On a practical level, that means you have a great deal of freedom. You don't have to raise your hand to speak. If you need to use the restroom, leave early for a doctor's appointment, or have some other type of emergency, you don't have to ask my permission. Just quietly get up and go. I won't penalize you.

Nor will I penalize you for being late to class once in a while, or even being absent, beyond the natural penalties that accrue as a result of your missing class time and activities. Unlike some of your other professors, I will not withdraw you from the class for excessive absences. If you want to withdraw, you'll have to do it yourself before the deadline. Otherwise, if you simply stop coming, you'll wind up with an F in the course.

You should also know that, according to several recent studies, students who attend class regularly earn, on average, one full letter grade higher than students who attend only sporadically. If you don't know what "sporadically" means, you should definitely come to class.

Along with considerable freedom, being an adult also carries a great deal of responsibility. You're responsible, first of all, for displaying good manners, being considerate of others, and generally not being a jerk. That means you won't interrupt other speakers, including me. You won't routinely be late to class, or regularly leave before it's over, because that's rude. And you'll keep your cell phone turned off, unless you have some really good reason to leave it on, such as your mother is in the hospital, your partner is about to give birth, or the Braves are playing in the World Series (like that ever happens).

Moreover, you are personally responsible for everything we cover in class, whether you're here or not. I don't mean this unkindly, but please don't come to me and ask, "Are we going to be doing anything important on Wednesday?" Of course we're going to do something important on Wednesday. Otherwise, I wouldn't be here either.

And please don't ask, "Is it OK if I'm absent on Friday?" or "Is it OK if I leave early?" As far as I'm concerned, it's neither OK nor not OK. I prefer you to be in class all the time, for the simple reason that I want you to succeed in the course. But it's entirely your decision. You're an adult. Do what you have to do. You don't need my permission, nor will I give it. Just remember that you're responsible for all the material.

Likewise, please don't stop by the lectern before class to say, "Can you tell me what we talked about on Monday?" No, I can't. We talked about a lot of stuff on Monday, and I spent an hour and fifteen minutes doing it. There's no way I can recap that for you in the thirty seconds before class starts.

Besides, I did my part. I went over the material, as promised on the syllabus. It's now your responsibility. If you have a legitimate reason for your absence—not an excuse, but a reason—such as a documented illness, a death in the family, or the Braves losing to the Mets (which is kind of like a death in the family), then see me during office hours and I'll try to bring you up to speed. Otherwise, I recommend that you exchange email addresses with two or three classmates and agree to share information if one of you has to be absent.

Is everyone clear on that? In this classroom, we're all adults. I promise to treat you like an adult, and you agree to behave like one.

OK. Before we turn to the syllabus, let's go back briefly to the subject of grades. I'm sure many of you have seen the comments on RateMyProfessors saying that I don't give many As. That's true, I don't. And for a very good reason: There aren't many A students.

© totallypic/Shutterstock.com

If you'll look at the college catalog, you'll see that A stands for "excellent." The fact is, few students are truly excellent. I don't mean to hurt your feelings by saying that, because I know many of you have been told all your lives just how excellent you are. But you see, the root word of "excellent" is "excel," which means to surpass all others or to stand out. By definition, not everyone can surpass all others. If everyone stands out, no one does. (Anybody ever heard of Lake Woebegone? No? Never mind.) No doubt you are bright, as indicated by the fact that you're here. But it's unlikely that, as I begin evaluating your work, more than a few of you will actually stand out.

On the other hand, although not everyone can excel, a lot of people can be good. You may have also noticed, on that same RateMyProfessors page, a number of others commenters who said it was easy to get a B in my class. That's not a contradiction—although I wouldn't say it's exactly easy. But it's certainly very possible. Because, going back to the college catalog, B means "good." And if you're smart enough to get this far to begin with, you're probably smart enough to do well in the course, provided you show up and work hard. In other words, although only a few of you will legitimately excel, most of you can be good if you want to be, in which case I'll have no trouble assigning you a B.

Now that we have that settled, let's take a look at the syllabus. And by the way, just so you can adjust your expectations, I probably will keep you here the entire seventy-five minutes today. That way, when somebody shows up at the next class meeting and asks if we did anything in the first day of class, I'll be able to say, "Absolutely."

Reflection questions for "Welcome to My Classroom":

1. What does it mean to be an "adult," in the context of a college course?

    _____

    _____

    _____

    _____

    _____

    _____

    _____

    _____

2. What are some things you should do if you have to miss class one day—or if you just missed accidentally?

    _____

    _____

    _____

    _____

    _____

    _____

    _____

    _____

3.   What does an A grade actually signify?

_____

_____

_____

_____

_____

_____

_____

_____

_____

4.   What does a student typically need to do in order to earn a B?

_____

_____

_____

_____

_____

_____

_____

_____

_____

2

A Philosophy of Teaching

Most teaching statements are written by people who—let's be honest—don't really know that much about teaching. Usually the writers are first-time job seekers with, at best, a year or two as a graduate assistant or an adjunct under their belts.

Battle-scarred classroom veterans, unless they happen to be going on the market, rarely write a statement of teaching philosophy. But maybe they should.

My philosophy of teaching has been forged over more than thirty years, twenty-eight of those years as a full-time instructor. As a student, I attended a private liberal-arts college and a midsized regional university. I've taught at a large land-grant university, a small rural community college, a large metropolitan community college, and a suburban technical college.

Like everyone in the profession, I came to the job with a number of preconceived notions, based partly on observations of my own teachers, both good and bad, and partly on my perception of how things should operate in a perfect world. Most of those notions proved false or impractical, and the jury is still out on the rest.

In addition, since I also spent more than ten years supervising faculty members, my teaching philosophy has been profoundly influenced by my experiences with colleagues. I've had the great fortune to observe and learn from some of the best teachers in the world. I've also known a few faculty members whose chief contribution to my development was to strengthen my resolve never—*ever*—to do certain things.

Please note that in sharing my philosophy, I'm not suggesting that it's the definitive approach or encouraging anyone else to adopt it. I'm simply sharing what I've come to believe.

College students are adults. I wrote about that truism in my earlier essay, "Welcome to My Classroom," but it bears revisiting as one element of a more comprehensive philosophy.

People tend to rise or fall to the level that is expected of them. Make it clear that you think students are stupid and, odds are, they will underperform. Act like you expect them to misbehave, and your classroom will probably resemble a war zone. But if you tell students upfront that you consider them to be adults, and then treat them accordingly, most will attempt to live up to the label. That's certainly been the case in my classroom over the years.

Treating students like adults means you allow them the freedoms that adults enjoy—to be late for class, for instance, to miss it altogether, or to leave early if that's what they need to do. At the same time, you make it clear that, as adults, they are responsible for all the material in the course, whether or not they were in class on a particular day.

That approach has profound implications for every aspect of classroom management, from discipline to attendance to late papers. Students like it because they already think of themselves as adults and appreciate being viewed that way. (College students despise few things more than being treated as though they were still in high school—even if they are actually still in high school.) And it's good for professors because it shifts the responsibility for "keeping up" onto the students, where it belongs.

Teaching is performance art. I wish I had coined that phrase, or at least knew who did. I just know that it has become one of my foundational beliefs.

The concept of the teacher as performer, as "the sage on the stage," has fallen out of favor in recent years. But the fact is, we are sages and we are on a stage. How we perform—that is, how we teach—is every bit as important as what we teach.

Moreover, how our students respond to us—and by extension, to our subject matter—depends largely on the quality of the performance we give in class, day in and day out. Want to engage your students, capture their interest, motivate them to do more and be more? Then pay attention to voice inflection and body language, just as an actor would. Practice your timing. Play to your audience. Inject some humor. Entertain.

That doesn't mean you have to make yourself the focal point of the classroom all the time. Class discussions, group work, and other non-teacher-centric strategies can also be effective. But when the curtain goes up and it's your time to shine, go out there and knock 'em dead.

Great teachers may be born, but good teachers are made. The ability to become a great teacher—one who inspires students and seems to connect with them effortlessly—is a gift, an innate talent like musical ability or athletic prowess.

Just like any other gift, it can either be squandered or put to good use. The very best teachers are those who have the gift and have worked hard over many years to further develop it—although we often overlook the hard work because they make being a great teacher look so easy.

But what about those of us who may not have "the gift," or at least not to the same degree? Can we, too, become great teachers? Maybe not, but we can become good ones. Just as with any other skill, the key to becoming a

good teacher is to *want* to become one. My son will never play in the NBA, because he lacks certain genetic traits, such as extreme height and freakish athletic ability. But he became a fine high-school basketball player by studying the game, learning all he could from his coaches, attempting to emulate those who play it well, and spending hours honing his skills. The path to becoming a good teacher is no different.

You don't have to be a jerk. If you consistently place your ego and personal interests ahead of others' needs—even when those needs should be paramount—then you are a jerk. The teacher as jerk can take many forms: someone who never returns papers, who avoids office hours, who passes the buck on advising, who generally thinks that his or her time is more important than anyone else's.

There is also the more obvious type of jerk, the one who berates and embarrasses students in front of classmates; who responds to questions with superciliousness, arrogance, or even open contempt; whose default response to any situation is to take the extreme hard line.

When I was an administrator, I occasionally dealt with such faculty members, like the one who delayed a student's graduation an entire semester because he wouldn't accept a paper that was one hour late. I usually tried to reason with those people but often found them impervious to reason. In the end, if they had followed policy to the letter, I had to support them, but I didn't like it. I thought they were being jerks.

I'm well aware of the school of thought that says teachers have to behave like jerks for the sake of their students. The world is full of jerks, this philosophy goes—heck, most of their bosses will be jerks—so we as their professors have an obligation to cultivate jerkiness in order to prepare them for the real world. Hence the hardline approach, the overly strict interpretation of policy, the refusal to budge an inch.

I've never bought that philosophy. In my experience, most of the people who espouse it don't actually know anything about the "real world." They're just trying to justify being jerks. And I don't believe for a moment that they really have students' best interests at heart.

Occasionally a student does need to learn a hard lesson in personal responsibility. But every student needs a break now and then, and most of them won't ever get to those corporate jobs we're so worried about if we don't cut them some slack now and then.

Besides, I spend zero time worrying about whether students are taking advantage of me. My goal is to help students succeed while still holding them to a reasonable standard. If some take advantage and that ends up hurting them down the road—when a boss or perhaps another professor isn't quite as understanding—that's their responsibility, not mine.

All you need is love. Well, maybe that's not *all* you need to be a good teacher. It helps to have an advanced degree, and maybe some actual knowledge of the subject matter. But in teaching, as in other human relationships, a little love goes a long way.

When I talk about love, I mean, first and foremost, love for students. Of course you're not going to experience strong feelings of affection for each and every student, and that's probably just as well. There will be some students you don't like much at all. That's normal.

But a good teacher has a love for students in general, students as a group. I make that point because I've known so many teachers who seem to dislike students, even to hold them in contempt. You can tell by what they say about students in private.

Whenever I hear a faculty member constantly talking about how stupid or rude students are, I think to myself, "Then why are you doing this?" It's little wonder that their teaching ratings show that students don't care much for them, either.

Also when I talk about love, I'm referring to love of the subject matter. We've all had teachers who appeared bored with their own lectures, disenchanted with their assignments, and indifferent to class discussion. Then we've had teachers whose passion for their subject matter made us feel passionate about it, too. For many of us, it was the latter group who inspired us to become teachers.

Of course, even if you clearly love teaching, grant students adult status, give an Oscar-worthy performance every day, and resist your jerkier impulses, that doesn't mean your students will come to love your class. But at least maybe they won't hate it—or you—quite as much.

Reflection questions for "A Philosophy of Teaching":

1. How would you summarize the author's teaching philosophy?

_____

_____

_____

_____

_____

_____

_____

2. What does is it mean that "teaching is performance art"?

_____

_____

_____

_____

_____

_____

_____

3. In what ways can a teacher be a jerk? In what ways can a student be a jerk?

    _____

    _____

    _____

    _____

    _____

    _____

    _____

    _____

4. What role does love play in the teaching process?

    _____

    _____

    _____

    _____

    _____

    _____

    _____

    _____

Defining the Relationship

Dear Students: I think it's time we had the talk. You know, the one couples who've been together for a while sometimes have to review boundaries and expectations? Your generation calls this "DTR"—short for "defining the relationship."

We definitely need to define our relationship because, first of all, it is a long-term relationship—maybe not between you and me, specifically, but between people like you (students) and people like me (professors). And, second, it appears to need some defining, or redefining. I used to think the boundaries and expectations were clear on both sides, but that no longer seems to be the case.

The truth is, I wonder if college students today truly understand the nature of their relationship to professors. Perhaps their experiences with other authority figures—high-school teachers, parents, and bosses—have led them to make assumptions that aren't quite accurate. Or perhaps students are just not too thrilled with authority figures in general. That's always been the case, to some extent. But it seems to me, after 31 years of college teaching, that the lines have grown blurrier, the misconceptions more profound.

So I'd like to take a few moments to define the professor-student relationship. And if no one has ever put it to you quite this way before—well, that just highlights the need for a DTR.

And by the way, please keep in mind that I'm not trying to offend you or tick you off. I actually like you quite a bit, or I wouldn't even bother having this discussion.

I don't work for you. Students (or their parents), when they're unhappy with something I've said or done, occasionally try throwing this line in my face: "You work for me." They mean that by paying tuition and taxes, they pay my salary and I should, therefore, be responsive in the way they desire.

Let's dismiss that old canard right off the bat. Yes, as a professor at a state institution, I am a public employee. But that's precisely the point: I'm employed by the college and by the public, not by any particular member of the public. My duty—to the institution and to the people of this state—is to ensure that students in my courses meet the standards set by the college's faculty and are well-prepared for further study and for life.

You're not a customer, and I'm not a clerk. Unfortunately, too many students have been told for too long that they are "customers" of the institution—which means, of course, that they're always right. Right?

Wrong. This is not Wal-Mart. You are not a customer, and I don't even own a blue smock. Our relationship is much more like that of doctor and patient. My only obligation: to tell you what you need to hear (not what you want to hear) and to do what I think is best (not what you think is best).

I'm not a cable network or streaming site. Natives of today's social-media-fueled digital universe have come to expect that everything they want will be available whenever they want it, on demand. That includes, or ought to include, their professors. I mean, we have email, don't we? And cell phones?

Consider this official notice that I have opted out of the on-demand world. My office hours are listed on my syllabus. If for some reason I can't be in my office during those hours, I'll let you know beforehand if possible or post a note on my door. But I'm usually there.

As for email, yes, I have it and I check it often, but not constantly. I do have a life outside this classroom—a wife, kids, hobbies, other professional obligations. That's why I don't give out my private cell number. If you need me after hours, email me and I'll probably see it and respond within 24 to 48 hours.

I'm not a high-school teacher. A common refrain among first-year college students is, "But my high-school teacher said. ..."

Those teachers did their best to prepare you for college and tell you what to expect. Unfortunately, some of their information was outdated or just plain wrong. For example, not every essay has exactly five paragraphs, and it's OK, in certain situations, to begin a sentence with "because." One of the main differences between them and me is that I'm not telling you how you're going to do things "once you get to college." This is college, and this is how we do things.

Plus, because of something called "academic freedom," which most college professors enjoy but most high-school teachers don't, I'm not nearly as easy to intimidate when you think you deserved an A. I'm sure you (or your parents) would never dream of trying anything like that, but I thought I'd go ahead and mention it, just in case.

I'm not your boss. Please don't misunderstand: I don't take a "my way or the highway" approach to teaching. In my view, that's not what education, and certainly not higher education, is all about. I'm here to help you learn. Whether you choose to accept that help—ultimately, whether you choose to learn anything—is up to you.

My role is not to tell you what to do, like your shift manager at the fast-food restaurant. Rather, I will provide information, explain how to do certain things, and give you regular assignments and assessments designed to help you internalize that knowledge and master those skills. Internalizing and mastering are your responsibility. I can't "fire" you, any more than you can get me fired. But I can and will evaluate the quality and timeliness of your work, and that evaluation will be reflected in your final grade.

I'm not your parent. Some of my colleagues (especially among the administration) believe the institution should act "in loco parentis," which means "in the place of a parent." In other words, when you're away from your parents, we become your parents.

I've never really subscribed to that theory, at least not in the classroom. I suppose there are certain areas of the college, like student services, that have some parental-like obligation to students. But as a professor, I don't. And what that means, more than anything else, is that I'm not going to treat you like a child.

I'm not your BFF. When I first started teaching, I was only a few years older than many of my students. It was tempting, at times, to want to be friends with some of them. I occasionally struggled to maintain an appropriate professional distance.

Not anymore. I've been doing this for a while now—over 30 years—and I'm no longer young. (Sadly, I'm no longer mistaken for a student, either.) I try to be friendly and approachable, but if by "friendly" you think I mean "someone to hang out with," I don't. I regret that we cannot actually be friends.

That applies to virtual friendship, too. Even if you happen to track me down on Facebook, I will not accept your friend request. You're welcome to follow me on Twitter, if you like, but I won't follow you back. And I don't do Instagram or Snapchat or, um, whatever else there is.

I'm not your adversary. Just because we're not best buds, please don't think I'm your enemy. Nothing could be further from the truth. In fact, if by "friend" you mean someone who cares about your well-being and success, then I guess I am a friend after all.

Yet there is always a degree of tension in the student-professor relationship. You may at times feel that I am behaving in an adversarial manner—questioning the quality and relevance of your work, making judgments that you perceive as negative. Understand that is only because I do want you to succeed. It's not personal, on my end, and you must learn not to take it personally.

I'd like to be your partner. More than anything, I'd like for us to form a mutually beneficial alliance in this endeavor we call education.

I pledge to do my part. I will:

- Stay abreast of the latest ideas in my field.

- Teach you what I believe you need to know, with all the enthusiasm I possess.

- Invite your comments and questions and respond constructively.

- Make myself available to you outside of class (within reason).

- Evaluate your work carefully and return it promptly with feedback.

- Be as fair, respectful, and understanding as I can humanly be.
- If you need help beyond the scope of this course, I will do my best to provide it or see that you get it.

In return, I expect you to:

- Show up for class each day or let me know (preferably in advance) if you have some good reason to be absent.

- Do your reading and other assignments outside of class and be prepared for each class meeting.

- Focus during class on the work we're doing and not on extraneous matters (like whoever or whatever is on your phone at the moment).

- Participate in class discussions.

- Be respectful of your fellow students and their points of view.

- In short, I expect you to devote as much effort to learning as I devote to teaching.

What you get out of this relationship is that you'll be better equipped to succeed in this and other college courses, work-related assignments, and life in general. What I get is a great deal of professional and personal satisfaction. Because I do really like you guys and want the best for you.

All in all, that's not a bad deal. It's a shame more relationships aren't like ours.

Reflection questions for "Defining the Relationship":

1. How is a college professor different from a boss? From a parent?

_____

_____

_____

_____

_____

_____

_____

2. In what ways can students and professors be friends? In what ways can they not?

_____

_____

_____

_____

_____

_____

_____

3. In the professor-student "partnership," what should professors do?

_____

_____

_____

_____

_____

_____

_____

4. What should students do?

_____

_____

_____

_____

_____

_____

_____

Day One of the Semester

One of the things I love most about teaching is the constant sense of renewal, of beginning afresh. College professors get to experience that twice a year—more often, if they teach on the quarter system or in the summer.

Given the unique opportunity to constantly start over—with new classes and students, updated materials, maybe new classrooms and equipment—it strikes me that the first day of any class is the most important of the semester. It's the meeting that sets the tone for the rest of the term, helping you get the course off to a great start.

Or not.

It is, of course, possible to overcome a bad first session. And even if your opening-day performance is brilliant, problems can crop up later on that make for a trying semester. But generally speaking, what happens on Day One—how you act, what you say, even how you look—will go a long way toward determining your relative success or failure as the instructor of that course.

You may be a brand-new teacher staring down your first-ever Day One. Or maybe you're a classroom veteran who hasn't been altogether satisfied with the way your semesters have started. Either way, here are some tips for a successful first day of class.

Be yourself. One of the biggest mistakes that inexperienced (and sometimes even experienced) teachers make is going in on the first day and acting like somebody they're not. Maybe they attempt to sound stricter than they really are, or make jokes they wouldn't normally make, or affect certain behaviors (borrowed from their own former professors) that don't come naturally for them.

That is a mistake because most students will see right through you. They'll know immediately and intuitively that you're putting on a show, and their subconscious interpretation will be that you're not altogether comfortable with yourself, that you don't really know who you are, and that you're therefore unreliable as an authority figure and dispenser of knowledge.

As for the students who do buy your act on Day One—well, they're going to be surprised, confused, maybe even a little angry when they discover down the road that you're not really who you suggested you were. And they will discover it. Nobody can keep up an act for an entire semester.

So don't be afraid to be yourself. If you're the no-nonsense type, then make that clear from Day One. If you enjoy self-deprecating humor, throw in a joke or two at your own expense. If you get a little cranky at times, then fine, be a little cranky. Students will be glad to know what they're getting themselves into. As long as you're consistent throughout the term, they are likely to tolerate whatever they perceive as your quirks or personality flaws.

Be yourself—but a little bit better. Being a *little* cranky is one thing. Later on in the semester, you might become a lot cranky, and the students will know to expect that. But try to rein in your inner curmudgeon a bit on the first day.

Likewise, you may fancy yourself a great comedian. OK. By all means, tell a few jokes. But don't try to turn the entire first class session into a stand-up comedy routine. You don't want to leave the impression that you're not serious about the course. Also, spending too much time trying to elicit laughs will probably prevent you from covering some important material.

Dress for success. The same advice applies to the way you dress on that first day: Be yourself, only a little bit better. If you normally teach in khakis and a button-down, try throwing on a tie or a scarf for Day One. If a tie is the norm, then maybe add a jacket. And if you like to dress up every day—well, I don't think I would recommend taking the next step and showing up in a tuxedo or a cocktail dress. A suit is probably formal enough.

Since I left administration, I've taken to wearing nice jeans (at least my wife says they're nice) and a neatly pressed button-down shirt. That is a comfortable "uniform" that suits my purposes as I roll up my sleeves and circulate among my writing students, often leaning against chair backs or squatting down beside desks to answer questions.

But on the first day of class, I usually wear khakis with my button-down. (I swore a solemn oath, when I returned to the classroom full time, never, ever to wear a tie.) That's being myself, just a slightly better version of myself. And the students aren't exactly shocked when I show up in jeans on Day Two.

What you don't want to do is wear a suit on the first day, then revert to jeans and a polo thereafter. Students find that kind of inconsistency confusing and maybe a little alarming, at least on a subconscious level. Again, don't be afraid to be more or less yourself in the way you dress, even if you do smooth out the rough edges a little.

Strike the right tone. I don't believe this piece of advice contradicts any that I've offered above. Being yourself doesn't necessarily mean winging it. You may still need to work on your presentation.

Edgar Allan Poe argued that there is only one acceptable tone for poetry: "melancholy." There really isn't one acceptable tone for college professors on the first day of class. (And even if there were, it certainly wouldn't be melancholy. We save that for the final exam.)

Different teachers use different tones on Day One because our personalities are different. Still, I think there are some basic elements of tone for which you should strive. Try to come across as confident, fair, reasonable, approachable (even if a bit curmudgeonly), and open-minded. And you should do so not because you're putting on an act, but because those are all appropriate professorial attitudes that you either genuinely embrace or are working hard to acquire. Try to avoid sounding pompous, arrogant, or dictatorial.

The Day One tone that works well for me, and that fits with my personality, is one I would describe as "amiable but no-nonsense." My objective is to let the students know that, although I take the course seriously, and I take them and their concerns seriously, I don't take myself overly seriously.

Convey key information. Perhaps the most important thing to do on Day One is to go over your syllabus and hit all the key points. You don't have to walk students through the entire document—much of it they can read for themselves. And you definitely don't need to project your syllabus up on the screen and read it aloud, word by painful word. You'll have students lining up at the registrar's office to drop before you get to page two.

There are three main things that students want to know on the first day of class: what they're going to be expected to do, how their final grades will be determined, and what the instructor's policies are regarding attendance, makeup work, etc. I always try to include a short speech on plagiarism and a little bit of my philosophy on teaching writing, although I generally save most of the latter for Day Two. But whatever else I do, I make sure to cover those three main items on the first day.

It's vitally important if you have your own policies governing classroom conduct to put those policies in writing *and* take the time to go over them in detail on Day One. That is especially important if your policies might be perceived as stricter than those of other professors. Students will appreciate the heads-up even if they don't care much for the policies. More important, should a particular policy come into dispute at some later point in the semester, you have the excellent defense that you not only put the rule in writing but covered it thoroughly on the first day of class.

Following all of those guidelines will not guarantee that you have an awe-inspiring opening day, much less that you will be successful in the rest of the course. But they should at least help you get off on the right foot, and that usually has a positive impact on the rest of the semester.

And even if things don't turn out as well as you might like this term, the beauty of teaching is that you always have the opportunity to make a few adjustments and start all over again next semester.

Reflection questions for "Day One of the Semester":

1. Why is the first day of class so important?

_____

_____

_____

_____

_____

_____

_____

2. What does it mean to "be a better version of yourself"?

_____

_____

_____

_____

_____

_____

_____

3. How does the instructor's tone impact the first day of class and beyond?

_____

_____

_____

_____

_____

_____

_____

4. What types of things should instructors cover on the first day of class?

_____

_____

_____

_____

_____

_____

_____

Welcome to My Classroom: ESSAYS ON THE FIRST YEAR OF COLLEGE

"I'm Not Paying for Your Opinion"

Perhaps, to explain Richard Arum and Josipa Roksa's now infamous findings in their landmark book *Academically Adrift: Limited Learning on College Campuses,* we need look no further than the current customer-service culture. That thought came to me after a recent incident in my introductory rhetoric course.

We were talking about the way that social mores and public opinions change over time, and how writing both influences and reflects those changes. When I broached one particularly controversial topic, a student interjected, "But that's just your opinion, and I'm not paying for your opinion."

OK, then.

In fact, I had not been expressing a personal opinion; rather, I was exploring a variety of other people's opinions and inviting students to evaluate them critically. But that's really beside the point. The more I think about the episode, the more I realize just how wrongheaded that student's comment was on so many levels.

For one thing, there's nothing that says students have a right to be shielded from opinions they don't like, or even a right not to be offended. Generally, I'm pretty careful what I say; I'm not a proponent of the "shock jock" school of pedagogy, intentionally setting out to provoke or offend students—although I know people do who teach that way, including some of my former professors.

However, it's virtually impossible to talk about important issues like race, gender, religion, sexuality, evolution, abortion, or justice (just to name a few) without saying something—or assigning some reading, or making some allusion—that someone might perceive as offensive. (Try asking a bunch of future nurses to read Jonathan Swift's "A Modest Proposal.") Yet it's a vital part of their education for students to read and think and talk about such issues, examining their own beliefs and assumptions in light of what great thinkers past and present have had to say. That's a major part of what we mean when we use the term "critical thinking."

Students also need to learn that being offended is an emotional response, not a rational one. If you don't like something I've said—or, as in this case, something somebody else said—don't just get upset about it. See if you can formulate a cogent rebuttal. That, too, is a key element of critical thinking.

Finally—and most importantly—students should understand that they are in fact paying for our opinions. That's not to say faculty members should necessarily be telling students *what* to think, but we do have a responsibility to teach them *how* to think. And that involves, in part, exposing them to what others have thought—including, when appropriate, ourselves.

The truth is that much of what I say in class, from the points I make about literary works to the way I teach argumentative writing, is (objectively speaking) a matter of opinion. Or, if we're not comfortable with the word "opinion," perhaps we can call it "professional judgment." Certainly, it's informed opinion, based on decades of training, study, and experience; in many cases, it's probably consensus opinion, reflecting the best minds in my field. But in the final analysis, it's still opinion.

And there's nothing wrong with that. Ultimately, that is what students are paying us for: not just what we know, but what we think about what we know, the well-tended and painstakingly-harvested fruits of our long intellectual husbandry.

Yet somewhere along the line, students seem to have acquired the notion that college professors are supposed to be mere dispensers of knowledge, functioning as a sort of human Wikipedia—or at least, the way they imagine that Wikipedia functions, not realizing, perhaps, how much of what's posted there is ultimately someone's opinion.

Additionally, the current emphasis on "customer service" in academe seems to have given some students the impression that they have the right to "purchase" only those ideas that they personally agree with, and that all other ideas or opinions are at best irrelevant and at worst akin to faulty products or unsatisfactory service.

No wonder Arum and Roksa found that so many students aren't developing critical-thinking skills in college. How can they, when the culture tells them that they don't have to grapple with ideas they don't like—ideas that, in their minds, they're "not paying for."

Reflection questions for "I'm Not Paying for Your Opinion":

1. Why is it important for students to consider other people's opinions?

_____

_____

_____

_____

_____

_____

_____

2. What does it mean that "being offended is an emotional response, not an intellectual one"?

_____

_____

_____

_____

_____

_____

_____

3. In what way are students actually paying for their professors' opinions?

_____

_____

_____

_____

_____

_____

_____

4. How has the emphasis on "customer service" influenced the way college students view their classes and professors?

_____

_____

_____

_____

_____

_____

_____

The Rules about Classroom Rules

During his 1983 NCAA championship run, legendary North Carolina State basketball coach Jim Valvano was asked by a reporter if he held "bed check" when the team was on the road.

"Absolutely," replied Valvano. "In fact, I just checked last night, and would you believe every single bed was there."

That story, although perhaps apocryphal, illustrates perfectly the dangers of overzealous rule-making. Too many college classrooms, I fear, have come to resemble Hogwarts School under the iron-fisted reign of High Inquisitor Dolores Umbridge, with a new edict issued weekly in response to some minor or imagined transgression.

Before you get carried away with legalistic pronouncements in your classroom, you might want to take into account the following inviolable rules about making rules.

Don't make a rule you can't enforce. I know it annoys you when students are texting or listening to music on their phones during class. How dare they not pay attention to your wonderful lecture?

The question is: Can you stop them? College kids are pretty adept at surreptitious texting, not to mention hiding their ear buds under hair and hoodies. They've been doing those sorts of things since middle school. How do you plan to catch them, short of patrolling the room like some sort of angry test proctor on steroids?

Making rules that are difficult to enforce can quickly turn your classroom into a kind of mini-police state, where you spend more time playing "gotcha" with students than you do actually teaching them. And setting rules you can't enforce at all is even worse. Essentially, you're encouraging students to break the rules—since, if they do, you can't do anything about it anyway—thereby creating a culture of rule-flaunting that seriously undermines your authority as teacher.

Decide what you can tolerate. Effective classroom discipline is often a matter of trade-offs. Sure, there are behaviors you don't like. But what can you put up with in exchange for relative peace and productivity?

In my composition classes, students spend a great deal of time on writing activities designed to help them with whichever essay we're working on at that point. I allow them to use their laptops because it would be pretty silly to make them write everything by hand when they're so used to composing on the keyboard and when the final essays have to be produced on a word processor anyway.

In allowing them to use laptops and other devices, I understand that some of them will probably be updating their Facebook status instead of working on their essays. Of course if I see them doing it, I'll say something like "OK, guys, this is writing time, not Facebook time." But most of them will never get caught, because it's too easy to click back and forth between windows. That's something I'm willing to tolerate because I believe that, on balance, allowing laptops in class solves more problems than it creates.

Think of the victims. I say that tongue-in-cheek because the truth is that many of the behaviors we legislate against in our classrooms are actually victimless crimes. We often make a rule against something just because it annoys us—not because it's actually harmful to other students or detrimental to the learning environment.

Eating and drinking in class fall into that category (in a regular classroom, at least; a computer lab, where thousands of dollars' worth of equipment could be destroyed by a spill, is another matter). Who are the students really hurting by snacking on chips or sipping a soda in class, other than those of us who skipped breakfast?

At most, when they're munching instead of taking part in the discussion, texting instead of listening, or surfing the Web instead of working on their essays, they're only hurting themselves. As long as students do those things quietly, I don't really see them as discipline problems, certainly not to the point that I'm willing to take steps to prevent them. That could ultimately do more harm than good.

Consider the consequences. Another question you have to ask yourself before making any rule is: What will be the cost of enforcing it?

Coach Valvano understood that if he held bed check, he might very well catch one of his best players out too late and have to suspend him, perhaps costing the team a chance to advance in the tournament. We might debate the ethics of forgoing such a check, but we can hardly question the rationale. Clearly, enforcing a curfew might have led to unacceptable consequences for Valvano and the other members of the team.

As teachers, we often have to make similar calculations. If we become the technology and food police in our classrooms, snatching up illicit iPhones and bags of chips and snapping shut laptop lids, who exactly is being disruptive? Who is doing more damage to the learning environment? The one quietly sipping a soft drink or the one grabbing it out of hand?

Moreover, sometimes overzealous enforcement can create real problems for the instructor. Do you know if you're even allowed to confiscate students' expensive electronic equipment? What if you take a snack away from a diabetic student? Might you open yourself up to a lawsuit, or at least to a reprimand? Is it worth taking the risk?

Understand the big picture. Before you start legislating against particular behaviors, you need to become intimately familiar with your college's student and faculty handbooks as well as its policy manual.

In other words, you need to know exactly what you can and can't do in your classroom—and whether or not the administration will back you if you attempt to enforce a particular rule. The next-to-last thing you want to do is create a rule that is simply going to be overturned by your department chair or dean the first time a student complains. The very last thing is to have a rule that's going to get you dragged into court.

Stick to the "biggies." For all the reasons just cited, I would recommend that you have as few classroom rules as possible and that the ones you do have fall under one of two major categories: academic honesty and (truly) disruptive behavior.

The nice thing is that, in both cases, you probably won't have to create a rule at all. Your college almost certainly has rules and policies dealing with those issues that you can simply copy and paste into your syllabus. That way, you get to avoid being the bad guy while at the same time dodging the label of Umbridgesque rule-monger.

I recognize that there are situations that call for special rules, such as safety guidelines in a science lab or prohibitions against food and drink in a computer lab. But, again, institutional or departmental policies regarding those problems may already exist and should be clearly posted where all students who use those facilities can see them.

Communicate clearly. Whatever classroom rules you decide on, you need to make sure you publish them clearly on your syllabus and then see that every student has a copy. Many instructors also have students sign a form acknowledging that they received the syllabus and understand the rules.

But simply publishing the rules isn't enough. Go over them clearly and explicitly on the first day of class, with refresher sessions throughout the term as needed. I've found that, whereas a printed syllabus can be rather cold and impersonal, you can often take the sting out of rules by talking about them and explaining your reasoning.

Be consistent. The last rule of rule-making is that, if you have a rule, you must enforce it, regardless of the consequences. You can't hesitate, and you can't be selective in your enforcement. Otherwise, you might as well not have the rule at all—and you're right back to the point I began with.

A colleague once asked me if I have a policy on eating in class. "Absolutely," I replied. "I tell students to keep their mouths closed when they chew."

I think Coach Valvano would have been proud.

Reflection questions for "The Rules about Classroom Rules":

1. Should professors have rules in their classrooms? Why?

_____

_____

_____

_____

_____

_____

_____

_____

2. What is the danger of making a rule you can't enforce?

_____

_____

_____

_____

_____

_____

_____

_____

3. What can be some of the consequences of questionable rules?

_____

_____

_____

_____

_____

_____

_____

4. Why is it so important for professors to be consistent in enforcing the rules?

_____

_____

_____

_____

_____

_____

_____

You Don't Have to Be a Jerk

Never mind the headline of a recent *Chronicle of Higher Education* advice column—"Be Hard to Get Along With," by Scott Hippensteel—which left me wondering what kind of person would be intentionally hard to get along with. (I think we all know the answer to that.)

It was the tease that caught my attention: "Growing problems of classroom decorum mean faculty members have to get tough or sacrifice learning for all students." Really? What exactly are these "growing problems of classroom decorum"? I've been teaching college students for over three decades, and I can honestly say that they're not noticeably different now, in terms of behavior in class, than they were when I started. Only the specific distractions have changed.

I'd like to speak specifically to new and soon-to-be faculty members. No doubt many of you followed the exchange between Hippensteel and Anthony Aycock (who wrote the piece Hippensteel was responding to, "Don't Be Hard to Get Along With"), and wondering who's right and what you should do.

I'll acknowledge upfront that I tend to side with Aycock. In fact, a few years ago I wrote what might be considered a precursor to Aycock's piece, "The Rules about Classroom Rules." Like him, I was pilloried for allowing the barbarians through the gates.

But I'm not going to waste time trying to persuade experienced colleagues who are set in their ways. If they want to be hard to get along with, so be it. No doubt students need to learn to deal with people like that, since they're going to encounter enough of those folks in the workplace—especially if they go into higher education.

Just leave me out of it.

Because the truth is, you don't have to be a jerk or a "hard-ass" to be an effective teacher, and I want to make sure the rising generation of college professors understands that and is not misled into trying to become something they're not.

Remember, as I've written **more than once**, the key to being an effective teacher is to be yourself. If you are by nature a little hard to get along with, then OK—within reason, be hard to get along with. That's who you are. Students will adjust.

But most of us aren't like that, and faking it is both stressful for us and unfair to students, who are quick to pick up on pretense and can easily become confused. Ultimately, being a good classroom teacher has less to do with "getting tough" and more to do with being confident, competent, and engaging.

In more than thirty years of teaching, I've had only a handful of classroom behavioral problems, and only one that required any action on my part outside of class. The rest I handled easily right there in the room.

That's because maintaining classroom discipline is all about attitude. It's not a matter of making a bunch of rules, most of which you can't even enforce (even if you think you can), but of letting students know upfront that (a) you expect them to behave like adults and (b) you intend to treat them that way. You also have to know what you're talking about and, more important, *act* like you know what you're talking about, projecting an overall air of authority and no-nonsense good humor as opposed to arrogant nastiness.

And of course you have to be engaging. If students aren't paying attention, that's your fault. Yes, they have smartphones and iPads to distract them. But a generation ago they would have been doing their calculus homework or reading pulp fiction or playing hangman with their neighbor. Heck, I did those things as an undergraduate when I found my professors boring. But I can't remember ever not paying attention in my best professors' classes, which is largely what made them my best professors. (They also, incidentally, weren't hard to get along with.)

© Syda Productions/Shutterstock.com

Welcome to My Classroom: ESSAYS ON THE FIRST YEAR OF COLLEGE

If students aren't looking at you, then do something to make them look at you—like changing your vocal inflection, for instance. Or mixing in some discussion or small-group work. Or putting something interesting on the big screen to draw attention away from the little screens. Remember that teaching is performance art, and if that doesn't come naturally to you, then you might need to work on your approach.

You just don't have to change your essential personality. If you're a nice person (as I'm sure most of you are), then be a nice person. You can be easy to get along with and still be rigorous, still have high expectations, still assign people the grades they've earned. To whatever extent students need to be exposed to jerks, in order to help them learn to cope in "the real world," well, don't worry: You have plenty of colleagues to pick up your slack in that regard.

Never forget that there are also many nice people in the real world, thank goodness. Because what would be the point of going to college and pursuing a career if every single person you encountered along the way was hard to get along with?

Reflection questions for "You Don't Have to Be a Jerk":

1. What do you think Hippensteel is referring to when he talks about "growing problems with classroom decorum"?

_____

_____

_____

_____

_____

_____

_____

_____

2. Why do some professors believe they have to be "hard to get along with"?

_____

_____

_____

_____

_____

_____

_____

_____

3. How can professors maintain classroom discipline without being hard to get along with?

_____

_____

_____

_____

_____

_____

_____

_____

4. Why is it so important for professors to be engaging? What are some ways they can accomplish that?

_____

_____

_____

_____

_____

_____

_____

_____

Welcome to My Classroom: ESSAYS ON THE FIRST YEAR OF COLLEGE

Libertarians vs. Authoritarians

Who knew how polarizing the issue of classroom management could be? I certainly didn't, until I started getting emails and other comments in response to my essay in *The Chronicle of Higher Education* entitled "The Rules about Classroom Rules."

Clearly, there are two distinct schools of thought regarding how best to manage one's teaching environment: the "libertarian" approach, which basically allows students to behave more or less as they like as long as they're not disturbing others, and what I'll call (at the risk of much additional abuse) the "authoritarian" approach, which calls for strict rules and swift punishments.

Consider the very first response to my essay, a long and (I thought) rather nasty comment in which the writer basically accused me of being single-handedly responsible for the decay of America's youth because I don't snatch up students' cell phones whenever I see them texting in class. My reply, I admit, was hardly kinder (OK, it was pretty snide): "Do you also require your students to sit up straight, raise their hands before they speak, and form a perfect line when they go to lunch?" Obviously, the person who wrote that comment and I are diametrically opposed on this issue, and we're both fairly snippy about it.

But here's the interesting thing: the comment on the *Chronicle's* website received fifty-four "likes," while my reply got thirty. If you're a regular reader of *The Chronicle* online, you know that very few comments earn more than a handful of "likes." Double digits are fairly uncommon. So fifty-four is *a lot* of "likes," and for that matter so is thirty.

In other words, it's clear that readers felt very strongly about this topic, one way or another. Judging from the ratio of "likes," I'd say that we classroom libertarians appear to be outnumbered by the authoritarians about two to one. You'll see the same thing if you read all seventy-nine comments: about two-thirds of them are against me, while the other third agree.

After more than thirty years in higher education, eighteen of those as a chair, dean, or program director, that doesn't exactly surprise me—although I was a bit taken aback by the vitriol apparent in some of the comments.

It's not that I don't expect academics to become a bit heated, at times, in defense of their viewpoints on various issues. It's just that I never anticipated that this might be one of those issues.

Please understand that I'm not taking sides. Well, maybe a little. Obviously, I think my more libertarian approach is better suited to the college classroom or I wouldn't have written about it the way I did. But I've also known many good teachers who took a more authoritarian stance. Heck, I studied under several of them, in both undergraduate and graduate courses.

The thing that does disturb me, though—if I may open another can of worms—is that I'm afraid a disproportionate number of academic administrators come from the authoritarian two-thirds of the faculty. That might explain the absence of true shared governance at most institutions, the rise of "insubordination" rhetoric that I've brought up in other essays, and perhaps some of the recent internal attacks on tenure that have made national headlines.

Reflection questions for "Libertarians vs. Authoritarians":

1. Define "libertarians" in the context of this essay.

_____

_____

_____

_____

_____

_____

_____

_____

2. Define "authoritarians."

_____

_____

_____

_____

_____

_____

_____

_____

3. What's the problem with the lack of civility apparent in this debate?

_____

_____

_____

_____

_____

_____

_____

4. If it's true that two-thirds of professors are more authoritarian, how does that affect administration?

_____

_____

_____

_____

_____

_____

_____

A Losing Battle

Not too long ago, I was rather publicly taken to task for **suggesting** that professors should not make classroom rules they can't enforce, especially governing the use of electronic devices.

"You're not teaching the students anything, they're not learning anything," wrote one reader. Said another, "The author acts as if you should just let all their bad behavior go." Several chimed in to affirm that they had banned all use of cell phones and laptops in their classrooms, gleefully boasting about the strictness of their rules and the severity of the consequences. They implied, or even stated outright, that by failing to take a similar approach I was contributing to the delinquency of America's youth and the decline of Western civilization.

In the first place, I've never been inclined to run my classroom that way. Moreover, as I've noted elsewhere, many of the "youth" that I'm supposedly leading down the primrose path are not really youth. In my suburban state college classrooms, at least, many of them are full-fledged adults, with jobs and families and lives outside of school.

As an adult with responsibilities of my own, I always have my cell phone with me, even during meetings—set on vibrate, to be sure, but if I got a text from my wife saying that my son had had a fender-bender or that the washing machine was flooding the basement, I would certainly respond. In fact, I would probably get up and leave. Why should I expect my adult students to behave any differently?

But the main point the electronics police don't seem to understand is that they are fighting a battle that they are bound, in time, to lose. More and more students are using their laptops and other devices for nearly everything these days, including taking notes in class. A cell phone is no longer just a cell phone. It's a microcomputer of its own, often containing important information—calendars, notes, even downloaded books—that students need to have with them in class. The same is true of a tablet computer, but even more so: It functions like a combination giant smartphone and mini-laptop.

Sure, all those devices can be misused, to text friends or check Facebook or surf the Net. So what. I used to sit in the back of the class and read *Lord of the Rings* or use my pencil and notepad to draw unflattering caricatures of my teachers. How are today's illicit activities so different?

To top it all off, textbook publishers are now marketing aggressively to handheld device users—and as a result, more and more students these days are downloading their textbooks onto their smartphones and iPads and Kindles. Since the e-version of a book is often half the price of the print version (or less), professors can hardly object without appearing churlish.

For that matter, many professors are playing along, putting their course materials on the Web and/or requiring students to use online tutorials such as MyMathLab. How can we tell them not to use their electronic devices in class when many of the resources we're giving them cannot be used any other way?

The fact is, we can't. And if we try, we're not only fighting a losing battle, but we're making ourselves look a little silly and old-fashioned in the process. Within ten years, if not sooner, the typical classroom will look much different than it did ten years ago, when the majority of the students sat there, pen in hand, textbook open to the side, dutifully taking notes on paper.

Instead, virtually all students will be taking notes and reading their assignments on a laptop. Or a smartphone. Or a tablet. Or something new, maybe some sort of hybrid device that hasn't even been invented yet.

As classroom teachers, we can either get on board that particular train or get run over by it.

Reflection questions for "A Losing Battle":

1. On what front, specifically, are professors fighting "a losing battle"?

_____

_____

_____

_____

_____

_____

_____

2. Why are they destined to lose the battle?

_____

_____

_____

_____

_____

_____

_____

3. What are some of the ways students use electronic devices for college these days?

_____

_____

_____

_____

_____

_____

_____

4. In what way is the college classroom different now than it was ten years ago? How will it differ ten years from now?

_____

_____

_____

_____

_____

_____

_____

Welcome to My Classroom: ESSAYS ON THE FIRST YEAR OF COLLEGE

10

Grades: What Are They Good For?

A recent experience involving a high-school student I know has led me to re-evaluate the way I, well, evaluate.

The student, an eleventh grader, brought me an English essay—excuse me, a language-arts paper—on which she had received a failing grade. She was devastated by the grade because she had never failed a writing assignment before. In fact, in her previous eleven years of public schooling, she had never made less than an A on any test or assignment in language arts, which, she told me solemnly (and her mother affirmed), was her "best subject."

(I confess: as I wrote that last paragraph, I could hear the collective voices of hundreds of my own students, protesting after getting Cs on their first writing assignments that they had "always made As in language arts." I could also hear myself responding, "This isn't high school anymore.")

In this case, there was some objective evidence that the young woman was an above-average writer. In addition to her stellar language-arts grades, she had won the state literary competition as a ninth grader and had published three or four editorials in the local newspaper. She also scored a perfect 5.0 on the AP World History exam, which included an essay.

That said, the paper in question was not an A paper, in my estimation. At least, I wouldn't have given it an A in my college courses. But then again, she didn't write it for a college course, but for a high-school class, and not even an AP class, at that. In any case, it was definitely *not* a failing paper. As a piece of writing it had much to recommend it, including some facility with language, few grammatical errors, and a distinct voice.

So why did her teacher give it an F? I scanned the comments and the attached rubric, trying to figure that out. And the best I could come up with was that the teacher was trying to send a message: "This is not tenth grade anymore. There's a new sheriff in town. Whatever you did to dazzle your other teachers won't work on me."

I didn't tell the student any of that. Instead, I gave her back her essay with what I hoped were a few helpful suggestions, along with some bromides about the teacher always being right. What she needed to do, I told her, was to figure out what this particular teacher wanted and then give it to her. No doubt she was less than satisfied. (What else could I say? I didn't want to throw that high-school teacher under the bus.)

But I came away from the experience wondering if I sometimes do the same thing—if I give grades to make a statement, or to get across a point, or to demonstrate my authority, rather than to let students know where they stand and how to improve. I try not to do that, but I'm probably guilty sometimes, just the same.

One of my favorite things about teaching writing at the state college level is that, for us, "freshman comp" is not a gatekeeper course. When I taught at a large land-grant institution, many years ago, I got the distinct impression that my job was not so much to teach students to write better but rather to determine who could already write well enough to remain at the university. In other words, I was a gatekeeper.

I've never felt that way at my two-year branch campus. I've always believed that my job is to help students learn to write and, therefore, pave the way for their future success in college and beyond. If my grading practices have not always reflected that philosophy, then that's something I need to think about and possibly rectify.

What Is a C? Grading essays involves a fair amount of subjectivity, as those of us who do it for a living know very well. It's not like feeding multiple-choice answer sheets through a Scantron machine. Even if you use a rubric, you still have to make a number of judgment calls: What exactly does "clear" mean? "Appropriate"? "Coherent"?

I'm often reminded of the time one of my fellow graduate students presented a seminar paper that he had written in reader-response style. At the time, back in the mid-1980s, I had never heard anything like it. I found it fascinating and thought it was pretty well done.

The professor, though, was not impressed. He was a venerable southern literary critic in the formalist tradition who, as a young man, had been associated with the Agrarians. Reader-response writing wasn't exactly what he was looking for in his seminar. He gave my friend a C. I remember wondering what might have happened if we'd had a different professor. Someone a little younger and less traditional might well have given that paper an A.

Of course grading essays from first-year college students is different, I think. There are, or should be, some basic standards upon which we all more or less agree. But I've found that those standards aren't always a lot of help when it comes to assigning letter grades. One person's B can still be other's C.

At the heart of the matter, I believe, lies the following question: What exactly is a C? My college's catalog, and probably yours, too, says that a C equates to "average." But what does "average" mean? Average compared to what?

After all, the seventh or eighth man on an NBA roster is, by definition, an average professional basketball player. But let him play down at the rec center for a couple hours on a Saturday afternoon, and he will absolutely dominate the competition. Clearly, "average" is a relative term.

So a C, when applied to our students, means average compared to…the general population? No, that doesn't make sense. Since only about a third of Americans get college degrees, most of our students are already above average compared to the general population. Average compared to college graduates? No, that's not fair, either. These students are just starting out.

The only reasonable comparison, it seems to me, is to other students at their exact same point in the educational process. And I don't just mean the other students in their class, or even in my other classes. I'm talking about all the students I've ever taught. That's their cohort, the group against which they must be judged, and in comparison to which they must be rated "average," "above average," or "below average."

In other words, after giving this matter a great deal of thought, here's what I've come to: The definition of "average"—and therefore of the C grade—is the bare minimum that I as an instructor have a reasonable right to expect of students when they walk into my classroom. After more than thirty years, I think I have a pretty good idea what that is.

My first-year composition students, who have presumably completed high school or earned a GED, should be able to write reasonably coherent sentences that contain relatively few major grammatical errors. They should know how to use verb tenses more or less consistently and make their subjects and verbs agree. They should have at least a basic familiarity with standard punctuation and mechanics. They should have some general sense of how to string sentences together to form paragraphs, and how to organize paragraphs into an essay.

Students who meet those criteria are, to me, the very definition of "average." Of course that doesn't mean that they can't get better over time and become "good" or even "excellent"; indeed, making that kind of improvement is (or should be) the point of taking the class. It's also true that my standards rise over the course of the term: I expect more from the second paper than from the first, and so on.

But a student who fulfills at least my minimum expectations will earn no worse than a C on that assignment. One who significantly exceeds those expectations will earn a B, maybe even an A. If a piece of writing does not rise to the level that I believe I have a reasonable right to expect, then I will assign it a D or perhaps even an F. (Although I rarely give Fs unless students simply fail to do their work. My college requires at least a C in freshman comp before students can move on, so a D is sanction enough without, perhaps, being quite as discouraging.)

When I'm grading an essay, then, I'm always asking myself a series of questions: Does it meet expectations? To what extent? Clearly? Just barely? Does it go beyond what I would expect of students at this stage? How far? Does it fail to meet expectations at all? Then I assign a grade based on the answers. I use numerical grades because they're easier to average and to indicate where the essay falls within the letter-grade range—72, for example, would be a low C, 74 or 76 a mid C, 78 a high C—but I always start, in my mind, with letter grades.

Vitamin B. According to the website Livestrong.com (yes, my students' research habits are rubbing off on me), carrots are an excellent source of vitamin B. I think about that sometimes when, as a writing instructor, I hold out the B grade as a kind of carrot before the horse, to use a hoary old metaphor.

Okay, so in this case it's also a pretty tortured metaphor. But I think you get my drift: I use the B grade, whenever possible, to try and motivate my writing students to learn and achieve more than they might otherwise.

My basic philosophy is that not everybody can get an A—more on that in my next essay—but most students are capable of getting Bs if they work hard enough. True, statistically speaking, most of them are C-level writers, but I make it clear from the beginning of the class that I'm going to do everything in my power to make it possible for them to get Bs.

I don't try to accomplish this by lowering my grading standards on their essays. Instead, I do it by requiring a great deal of writing beyond the graded essays—much of which may contribute to those essays, such as rough drafts—and then giving students points for simply completing the assignments. At the end of the term, I figure those points in with their essay grades, creating the very real possibility that someone with all Cs on his or her papers could earn—and I do mean *earn*—a B in the course.

My hope and belief is that, as they do all that "extra" writing—all those journal entries and rough drafts and so forth—they'll actually improve as writers, and that generally seems to be the case. Often a student who starts out making low Cs, but who really reaches for that carrot, ends up making high Cs and sometimes even low Bs by the end of the term. In those cases, even though the student's final average may still be a C, I'm happy to give him or her a B. That, in my estimation, is a grade well spent.

Of course, the problem with this philosophy is that a lot of students these days aren't interested in striving for a B. They expect to have As handed to them just for showing up. But I've found that, at a branch campus of a state college, a good number of my students are nervous about taking "English" and don't really expect to do well. For them, knowing that a B is a realistic possibility often does serve as an incentive to work a little harder. And even the students who expect an A (but aren't A writers) feel better about a B than they would about a C—assuming they do the work. If they don't do the work, it's easy to show them why they got a C.

"Do You Ever Give A Grades?" Speaking of annoying questions students ask, I was returning essays a couple of months ago when one of my students blurted out, "Do you *ever* give A grades?"

In point of fact, I do. Seven students in that very section (out of twenty-three) actually got As, not just on the assignment but for the course. Of course it was a bit of an unusual class, with a number of dually enrolled students (that is, advanced high-school students). I don't usually see that many As in a single section. So I guess it was a fair (if slightly annoying) question from a student who obviously didn't get an A himself.

The pat answer is that professors don't "give" As; students have to earn them. And of course that's true. But a better answer is that, no, in a first-year writing course at a branch campus of a state college, not many students typically get As. That has to do with the meaning of the A grade and with the nature of the course itself.

I've talked about this before, but let me review my philosophy here. The catalog definition of an A at my institution, as at most, is "excellent." But what does it mean to be "excellent," or to "excel"? It means literally to stand out, to rise above, to surpass. By definition, not everyone can excel. If everyone stands out, then no one does.

I think that's especially true in a skills-based course such as writing, where a certain amount of innate ability is required in order for someone truly to set oneself apart from the crowd. (I imagine much the same thing is true in performance courses like music and art.) As I mentioned in the previous essay, most students can become proficient, or good, writers if they're willing to work hard enough. But most are not excellent writers and will not become excellent writers over the course of a single semester.

In that sense, a writing course is much different from a knowledge-based course such as algebra. Although hardly a gifted mathematician, I was able to make an A in college algebra by studying my tail off, doing all the homework, asking questions in class, and getting additional help when I needed it, which was often. (I don't doubt that, in more advanced math courses, it also takes a certain amount of talent for students truly to distinguish themselves.)

Many of my students don't understand this difference, even though I attempt to explain it to them early in the semester. A couple of emails I received after the most recent semester ended should serve to illustrate my point. A lot of you have probably gotten emails like these. One student asked why she had received a B instead of the A she wanted, when she had worked so very hard. Another wanted to know why he hadn't gotten an A, even though, as he put it, "I made Bs on almost all my papers."

To the first, I responded that, while I appreciated her hard work, in the end the final grade must reflect mastery, not effort—especially at the A level. Through her diligence, she had become a much better writer than when she entered the course—in truth, she had progressed from a C writer to a B writer—but she had not become an exceptional writer, an A writer, either in terms of her final average or her level of mastery at the end of the semester.

To the second, I just said—well, I'll let you supply your own punchline.

Reflection questions for "Grades: What Are They Good For?":

1. What role do grades play in college courses? Why are they important—or not important?

_____

_____

_____

_____

_____

_____

_____

_____

2. What does it means to say that a student's work is "average"?

_____

_____

_____

_____

_____

_____

_____

_____

3. Is it true that most students can be good, but few can actually excel? Why or why not?

_____

_____

_____

_____

_____

_____

_____

4. What does it mean to say, "Professors don't give As; students earn them"? Is that true? Why or why not?

_____

_____

_____

_____

_____

_____

_____

11

Toward a Rational Response to Plagiarism

Plagiarism is making us crazy. No, the mere thought of plagiarism is making us crazy. Collectively, as a professoriate, we're obsessed with it.

Consider the essay, "The Shadow Scholar," an anonymous confessional by a man who purportedly produces student papers on demand. Originally published in *The Chronicle of Higher Education* in November 2010, it stood for more than a year as one of the most-viewed articles on that publication's website, garnering more than 600 comments. More recently, we all read with fascination *The Chronicle*'s account of Panagiotis Ipeirotis, a professor who got into hot water at New York University for blogging about the hordes of alleged cheaters in his courses (see "NYU Professor Vows Never to Probe Cheating Again—and Faces a Backlash, " July 2011). That piece, too, was among the site's most popular.

Yet all this preoccupation with plagiarism does little to help us answer the fundamental question: What can we as individual faculty members do about it?

My approach to student plagiarism over the course of my thirty-plus-year teaching career has been simple but, I believe, effective. I use strategies well known to most experienced professors, with a few twists of my own. Please note that what I'm about to describe is strictly my personal approach and does not reflect the official policies of my college (although I don't believe it conflicts with those policies, either).

Keep your priorities straight. I'm a writing instructor, not a detective. My primary responsibility is to help students learn to write better. Identifying and punishing plagiarists is, unfortunately, part of the job, but it is far from the most important part.

Of course I care about plagiarism, and I certainly take steps to deal with plagiarists once I have sufficient proof. But I don't spend an inordinate amount of time worrying about plagiarism or trying to catch students at it. I'd prefer to direct my time and energy toward something more positive, such as actually teaching the subject

I've been hired to teach. I'm not sure I can be both an effective writing teacher *and* a zealous anti-plagiarism crusader.

That's what Mr. Ipeirotis concluded, after his campaign to eradicate plagiarism in his courses at NYU backfired. As he wrote on his blog, "The whole dynamic of the class changes. [Students] hear what I'm saying, but back in their mind they are thinking about cheating, cheating, cheating ... It's a vicious cycle. So, I get into class—I'm less happy because I had to deal with cheating the day before, instead of preparing better for the class. Students get less happy. ... I don't get positive feedback."

State your policy in your syllabus. You need to discuss plagiarism with your students, and the best place to start is with a clear and comprehensive statement in your syllabus. That should include a definition and a list of potential penalties. If your college already has such a statement, use it; otherwise, write your own, but make sure that any penalties are in keeping with existing campus policies. No point making threats you can't enforce.

Your policy will serve both as a guide to students, letting them know what plagiarism is and what can happen to them if they commit it, and as a kind of contract with them. It's something you can point to later, if you have an actual case of plagiarism, as long as you stick to the policy as written.

© Jacek Dudzinksi/Shutterstock.com

Welcome to My Classroom: ESSAYS ON THE FIRST YEAR OF COLLEGE

Talk about it openly. Speak candidly about plagiarism on the first day of class. Begin by explaining clearly what it is, because a surprising number of students honestly don't know. In elementary school, they copy their reports directly from encyclopedias and other sources. By middle school they've learned to alter the wording so they're not "just copying." Perhaps in high school they're exposed to concepts of research and documentation.

But many students, when they arrive on our campuses, have not yet mastered those concepts or come to understand fully the difference between what they did in middle school and what we're asking them to do. We have to explain it to them, thoroughly—and not just on the first day of class but throughout the semester.

We also need to articulate the reasons that plagiarism is wrong: because it's a form of stealing, because it's unfair to other students, and because it ultimately prevents you from acquiring the writing skills you're going to need—and be expected to have—as college graduates in the workforce. In my experience, those reasons make a lot of sense to students. That doesn't mean some of them won't plagiarize anyway, but studies suggest that students whose professors discuss the subject directly are somewhat less likely to cheat.

In your discussion, don't dwell on the negative—on the penalties for cheating. But it doesn't hurt to mention them briefly. Knowing what might happen if students plagiarize can serve as a deterrent to those not swayed by moral arguments.

Above all, tell students explicitly that you expect them *not* to cheat. Even today, the teacher is still an authority figure. Your words carry more weight than you realize.

Make plagiarism difficult. One of the best ways to discourage cheating, as many researchers have concluded, is simply to design tests and other assignments that are difficult to cheat on.

That is easier with written assignments than with, say, multiple-choice tests. It's nearly impossible, for instance, to plagiarize an essay written in class with the teacher watching closely—assuming the teacher is actually watching closely. Out-of-class writing assignments are, of course, much more susceptible to cheating, but even then you can take steps to make it hard to cheat.

One of the most effective is to require multiple drafts, checking—if not actually grading—each to make sure that it represents further development of the previous draft. Personally, I'm not a big fan of in-class essays, for reasons I'll go into later. But I do often have students write first drafts in class. By comparing those drafts to subsequent drafts written out of class, I can make sure they aren't just buying canned essays off the Internet and that the original ideas, at least, are their own.

Another well-established strategy is to design assignments that don't easily lend themselves to canned essays. One of my favorite requires students to find a recent newspaper editorial on a topic of interest to them, and write a response. For a fiction or poetry analysis, I'll have students choose something from a recent journal or literary magazine. Any student can find an essay about "The Lottery" online, and a clever student might even be able to rewrite it to avoid detection by anti-plagiarism software. But it's pretty unlikely that even the cleverest student can find an essay about a short story published in the spring 2009 issue of *Ploughshares*.

Don't penalize the non-plagiarists. Whatever you do to discourage cheating, make sure you don't damage the integrity of the course or make it more difficult for students to learn. I think it's both wrong and counter-productive—not to mention incredibly cynical—to assume that every student is a plagiarist, whether nascent or full blown. You should start each course believing that most students are basically honest and genuinely want to learn. Otherwise, why would you stay in this profession?

I mentioned that I'm not a fan of in-class essays. That's because I teach students that good writing requires a great deal of time—time spent planning, writing, editing, and revising. Asking students to condense that process into a single class period is a little like requiring a surgical resident to perform a heart transplant in an hour.

For me, using in-class essays solely as a means of ensuring that students don't cheat is out of the question. I believe that would do great damage to the integrity of my course, in that I wouldn't be teaching students what I'm really trying to teach them. Ultimately, I would be the one doing the cheating—cheating students out of the educational experience they're paying for and have a right to expect.

What about the software? You may be wondering why I haven't said much about popular plagiarism-detecting software, like Turnitin.com. That's because I rarely use it.

I'm not a fan of the software. I understand why so many of my colleagues tend to rely on it heavily, but I don't, for three reasons. First, it seems to me that having students submit all of their essays through Turnitin or something similar is tantamount to saying that all of them are cheaters—or at least they would be, given the chance. I think that's a bad way to begin a teacher–student relationship. Second, the software doesn't do anything to deter common low-tech forms of plagiarism, such as students' getting others to write their essays for them. And finally, as Mr. Ipeirotis discovered, tracking students through software can become its own kind of obsession, distracting you from other, perhaps more useful, pursuits.

Let it go. If some students take unfair advantage of the fact that I let them do most of their writing outside of class, or that I don't use Turnitin, so be it. It's not that I don't care. I do, and if I catch them plagiarizing, I try to make sure that justice is swift and sure. I just don't devote an inordinate amount of my time to catching them—or to obsessing over the ones I don't catch.

When I say "let it go," I mean that in the metaphysical sense. I'm not saying you should ignore clear cases of plagiarism. But the truth is, there aren't many clear cases of plagiarism. Most cases are borderline, at best. It's also true that, no matter what you do to deter cheating, some students are going to find a way around it. You can go crazy thinking about that all the time.

It comes down to this: Either you can be a teacher or you can be the plagiarism police. I choose to be a teacher. As such, part of my job involves catching the occasional plagiarist. When that happens, I chalk one up for the good guys. Otherwise, I don't worry about it. I find that I'm much happier and more productive that way. True, some students may "get away with" cheating, for the time being, but I believe they'll get their comeuppance eventually.

After all, it's pretty hard to plagiarize a quarterly report.

Reflection questions for "Toward a Rational Response to Plagiarism":

1. Why is the author specifically advocating for a "rational" response? What is irrational about professors' typical response?

   _____

   _____

   _____

   _____

   _____

   _____

   _____

2. What does it mean to be "a writing teacher, not a detective"?

   _____

   _____

   _____

   _____

   _____

   _____

   _____

3. Why is plagiarism wrong?

_____

_____

_____

_____

_____

_____

_____

4. What can professors do to prevent it?

_____

_____

_____

_____

_____

_____

_____

12

Fifty First Days

Today was my first day of school—for the fiftieth consecutive year. I've been starting classes around this time every year since I first set foot in Miss Martin's kindergarten class, back in 1966. Sometimes I feel like I just went off to school one day and never came back. I've been in school ever since.

There are a lot of things I love about my job, and I'm grateful to have a job that allows me to do so many of the things I love. But what I love most, I think, is the constant sense of renewal that comes with starting afresh each August or September. For me as a college professor, the beginning of the school year is always a time of excitement and anticipation, filled with limitless possibilities—exactly as it was for me as a student in elementary school, junior high (not "middle school"), high school, college, and graduate school.

There may be other days, after the first one, that seem less exciting, less filled with possibility, but that first day is always one to anticipate.

People ask me sometimes if I ever feel burned out. After all, I've been teaching essentially the same stuff for over thirty years. The answer is no, I don't feel burned out (at least not yet), because even though it's "the same stuff," it's really not the same. I may be teaching the same courses every year, according to the catalog description or course-numbering system, but they're always different in substantive ways: new classrooms, new technologies, new reading selections, new strategies that I read about or learned at a conference and want to try out. To paraphrase the old Chinese proverb, you can never really teach the same course twice.

If nothing else, the students are different, and that may be the best part. Because even as technology changes and fashions change and new buildings sprout up and I myself grow older, I find that there's a certain timelessness to the classroom. Walking in to meet a class for the first time, it could just as easily be 1996 as 2016—even though most of my students weren't even born in 1996. Today's students, just like their counterparts from two or three or five decades ago, are a little nervous, a little overwhelmed, a little afraid, a little shy—but mostly just excited.

And on the first day of class—any first day of class—that pretty well describes me, too.

Reflection questions for "Fifty First Days":

1. What does the author mean when he says, "Sometimes I feel like I just went off to school one day and never came back"?

_____

_____

_____

_____

_____

_____

_____

2. What is the source of the "constant sense of renewal" that the author describes?

_____

_____

_____

_____

_____

_____

3. What does the author mean when he says "you can never teach the same course twice"?

_____

_____

_____

_____

_____

_____

_____

4. How are students today different from students twenty or thirty years ago? How are they similar?

_____

_____

_____

_____

_____

_____

_____

© Khakimullin Aleksandr/Shutterstock.com

© Monkey Business Images/Shutterstock.com

Part II

Essays on Teaching and Learning

Our Students Need More Practice in Actual Thinking

During a recent meeting of a committee charged with reviewing my state's higher-education core curriculum, a committee member asked, "Do students really need two math courses?"

In a word, yes.

Admittedly, as an undergraduate English major, I may have asked the same question myself a time or two. And certainly it's true that, in the nearly three decades since I sweated through precalculus, I've never once had to factor an equation—nor, frankly, do I remember how. (Just ask my teenagers, who've occasionally been misguided enough to ask me for help with their algebra homework.)

But that's beside the point. What I couldn't see when I was sitting in those math classes, but now understand clearly, is that the cognitive demands they placed on me, as I struggled to think in new and unfamiliar ways, were invaluable to my intellectual development. For most of us, such realizations are part of growing up, just as we come to understand later in life that our parents were right all along to make us eat our peas.

Over a thirty-plus-year career, I've done my share of forcing nutritional fare down unwilling throats—both literally, as a father of four, and figuratively, as a two-year-college English professor. Each semester I face the bored looks, apathetic expressions, and hostile body language of students asking themselves—and sometimes asking aloud—"What am I doing here? I'm a [fill in the blank] major. Why do I have to take English?"

My first job is always to answer those questions (spoken or unspoken), to help students understand the relevance of writing and literature to their academic goals and ultimately to their future professional lives. Sometimes it's a hard sell—arms folded across chests tend not to unfold for weeks—but I set forth my arguments at the outset and reinforce them every chance I get. At the end of the semester, if students have caught even a glimmer of what it means to be a truly literate adult, I feel as if I've succeeded.

No doubt many of my colleagues who teach core courses in the hard sciences and the social sciences, in math and humanities and fine arts, can relate. Perhaps that's why I'm so dismayed to find that the liberal-arts curriculum—the so-called "core"—is under attack, especially at two-year schools.

Make no mistake: It is under attack, from legislators with no understanding of the aims of higher education; from administrators focused short-sightedly on the bottom line; from chamber-of-commerce types who read "college" as "work-force development"; and even from some of our own colleagues, advancing their narrow agendas.

No doubt similar battles rage on at colleges and universities across the country. But I believe the debate is especially troubling for those of us who work at access institutions, because teaching the core curriculum is what we do.

The issue isn't just protecting our turf: Even if we eliminated literature classes because they were viewed as "unnecessary," we'd still have plenty of composition sections to keep us busy. The real question is, are we going to send students on to upper-division courses, or out into the world, who simply are not as well educated as they could be? Because that's what we're really talking about here when we invoke the term "core curriculum." We're talking about what constitutes a true education, as opposed to vocational training.

A university education once consisted of four (or more) years of reading and studying the great works of history, philosophy, religion, science, mathematics, and the arts. Only after becoming thoroughly familiar with the collective learning of his world did a "bachelor" begin training for his chosen profession, like law or medicine, often by apprenticing himself to a highly regarded practitioner.

The last remaining vestige of that system—which may have been cumbersome but produced highly literate people—is the so-called core curriculum, which now occupies not even a full two years of a student's education. The rest, generally speaking, isn't education at all; it's training.

Don't get me wrong: A certain amount of training is necessary in any profession. Teachers, nurses, bank managers, engineers, doctors, lawyers, and police officers all need to be thoroughly trained in the day-to-day operations of their jobs. You wouldn't want your surgeon, scalpel in hand, pausing over your exposed abdomen and wondering where to make the incision, however well-educated that surgeon might be. You want him or her to have been thoroughly trained in exactly when, where, and how to cut, snip, and sew.

That's what training is: learning to perform routine functions efficiently without having to spend much time thinking about them.

Education, on the other hand, although complementary to training, is in many ways its antithesis. If the point of training is to teach people to act without having to stop and think, then the point of education is, expressly, to teach people to stop and think. What is thinking, after all, if not the cognitive processes involved in acquiring information, analyzing it, reaching conclusions based on those analyses, and then communicating those conclusions? In other words: reading, listening, observing, studying, pondering, speaking, writing. Those are precisely the intellectual activities required of students in the liberal arts.

Further, by studying history, literature, the sciences, mathematics, and the fine arts, students learn what the great thinkers (and not-so-great thinkers) who came before them—what Emerson called "the mind of the past"—have thought. That provides them with a solid foundation for their own thought processes, enabling them as they take in and process information on their own to benefit from the collective wisdom—and folly—of the ages.

In recent years, the term "critical thinking" has become a favorite buzz phrase of the education establishment. Administrators urge professors to "include more critical thinking" in their instruction; legislators and employers constantly decry the workforce's "lack of critical-thinking skills."

When those of us in the liberal arts hear that term, we often have to suppress a rueful smile. What people mean when they say "critical thinking" is really just "thinking," and we've been teaching that for years—when we're not fending off attempts by those same administrators and legislators to water down our courses and replace them with vocational training.

What do people expect from MBAs, accountants, engineers, or elementary-school teachers who haven't had significant exposure to Shakespeare, to Aristotle, to Newton, to Jung? Do we really expect them to be deep thinkers? They may have been thoroughly trained to perform the normal, daily functions of their jobs, but inevitably situations will arise that weren't covered in the textbooks—situations that will force them to have to think for themselves. What will they do then, when they've gotten through our colleges and universities with as little practice in thinking as possible?

I'm not suggesting that we should devote students' entire four years of college to reading Aristotle. I'm saying that we don't need to dilute, any more than we already have, the part of our educational system that's actually educational. Yes, students do need two math courses, at least, just as they need at least a couple of history courses, a couple of science courses, a literature course or two, and an art course. Those are as vital to the personal and professional success of a future bank manager as any upper-division accounting course.

I'm also saying that a focus on the liberal-arts core is even more important at access institutions—not less important—than at research universities. For one thing, our students often come to us even less grounded in those areas than students at four-year schools. In many cases, the first they'll ever hear of Sartre or Gibbon will be from us. We have a lot of ground to make up in a short time, with no courses to waste. Wherever our students are headed, whether off to a university or straight into the workplace, they deserve the best education—and not just the best training—that we can give them.

Those of us who teach in the liberal arts hold that truth to be self-evident; it's the reason we continue to do what we do. We can only hope that, in the midst of an economic crisis caused in large part by people behaving irrationally, those who hold the purse strings won't respond by eliminating the very courses and programs that could do the most to mitigate the problem.

Reflection questions for "Our Students Need More Practice in Actual Thinking":

1. Do college students need to take courses that have nothing to do with their major? Why or why not?

2. What are the similarities between education and training? What are the differences?

3. What does it mean to be "well-educated"—that is, what are the hallmarks of a well-educated person?

_____

_____

_____

_____

_____

_____

_____

4. What does critical thinking actually entail? Why is it important for students to be able to think critically?

_____

_____

_____

_____

_____

_____

_____

Welcome to My Classroom: ESSAYS ON THE FIRST YEAR OF COLLEGE

14

The Liberal Arts Are Workforce Development

Community colleges and other access institutions occupy a unique position in the national debate over the value of the liberal arts. But it's a position that is generally overlooked, if not ignored altogether.

For students who are not liberal-arts majors, the core-curriculum courses they are "forced" to take as freshmen and sophomores will probably constitute the extent of their dabbling in the liberal arts. Those who go on to study business, engineering, or computer science are unlikely, as juniors and seniors, to sign up for additional classes in literature, biology, psychology, or art appreciation.

Now consider that, according to the American Association of Community Colleges, about half of all freshmen and sophomores are enrolled at the nation's 1,300 two-year colleges, and many of those students transfer to four-year institutions. For a large percentage of people who earn bachelor's degrees, then, the liberal-arts portion of their education was acquired at a two-year college or similar access institution. Next, factor in all the community-college students who enter the workforce after earning two-year degrees or certificates, and whose *only* exposure to the liberal arts occurred in whatever core courses their programs required.

The conclusion becomes obvious: Two-year colleges are among the country's leading providers of liberal-arts education, although they seldom get credit for that role. Many Americans learn at a two-year college most of what they will ever learn—in a formal setting, at least—about writing, critical thinking, the history of our culture and civilization, the environment, and human behavior.

The reality that community colleges are actually liberal-arts institutions is at odds with the way two-year campuses are often portrayed in the media—and in government press releases—solely as engines of workforce development.

I wonder, though, if those seemingly conflicting views of the community-college mission are as mutually exclusive as they appear. Employers rank communication and analytical skills among the most important attributes they seek in new hires, according to the National Association of Colleges and Employers. Perhaps those of us who teach those very skills at community colleges should embrace the integral role we play in preparing the nation's workers rather than rejecting the idea of workforce development as somehow beneath us.

Such a paradigm shift would have at least a couple of happy consequences. For one thing, we would be able to argue more persuasively for the importance of the liberal arts, especially in this era of draconian budget cuts and increased oversight by external bodies.

More important, this new perspective could have a positive effect on student success. If we come to see ourselves as preparing students not just for transfer but ultimately for the workforce, then students may be more likely to understand the relevance of the skills we teach them and better able to use those skills for some purpose other than just getting a passing grade. That, according to Susan de la Vergne, a nationally recognized expert on preparing liberal-arts graduates for careers in non-liberal-arts fields, could give them a tremendous advantage.

"Businesses spend a lot of money on 'training' classes for their employees," she says. "Classes in business writing, presentation skills, business analysis, conflict resolution, emotional intelligence, and cross-cultural teamwork are deemed critical to success in today's business environment. But most are aimed at essentially backfilling the liberal arts, making up for education gaps."

Community-college faculty members are well positioned to help alleviate the need for so much "backfill." But to do so, we must reimagine the way that we teach. Here are a few suggestions that might help make our courses more practical, relevant, and useful for non-liberal-arts majors.

Require lots of writing. As the management guru Peter Drucker argued, communication is the one skill required of all professionals, regardless of field. "As soon as you take one step up the career ladder," he said, "your effectiveness depends on your ability to communicate your thoughts in writing and in speaking." Of course, the larger the organization, the more likely that the bulk of that communicating will involve writing. That has been true for years, but never more so than today, when practically every white-collar (or no-collar) worker in the country begins the day by checking and responding to email.

Meanwhile, the recent landmark book *Academically Adrift: Limited Learning on College Campuses* found that half of the students the authors surveyed had taken fewer than five courses that required twenty pages or more of writing. So in a world where degreed professionals are required to write more and more, apparently our institutions of higher education are asking students to write less and less.

Is there something wrong with this picture?

Clearly, one of the best things we can do for students is to require them to write—a lot. I understand that some faculty members teach large sections and can't grade four or five essays from each of their many students. But professors who administer nothing but multiple-choice tests are shortchanging their students. Instructors can assign and grade at least one or two writing assignments, or perhaps include a short essay as part of each test. They can also create writing assignments that don't have to be graded, in the traditional sense, such as journal

entries and online posts. Any writing is better than none at all, and writing that will be evaluated (if not graded) by peers may be the most useful of all.

Focus on critical thinking. A common complaint of employers, as reflected in the NACE survey, is that many workers have difficulty thinking for themselves. They may be thoroughly trained, having mastered all of the concepts in the textbooks, but, inevitably, situations arise that weren't covered in the books. When that happens, the ability to think critically, independently, and creatively becomes indispensable. Too many workers lack that ability, perhaps because, as *Academically Adrift* suggests, we're not emphasizing it enough in our college classrooms.

Sure, we've all had the "critical thinking" mantra drilled into our heads. But has it stuck? How many of us actually require our students to analyze material in an in-depth way (as opposed to providing them with convenient study sheets)? How many of us require them to draw inferences, make connections, question assumptions, reach and defend conclusions? Our liberal-arts courses are the ideal places to teach those cognitive skills that students need to be successful in the workplace. In fact, teaching that kind of deep thinking should be the hallmark of every liberal-arts course. That's what liberal-arts courses do best.

Bring the real world into the classroom. Another strategy we can adopt, if we want our courses to be more relevant, is to make our class discussions, case studies, experiments, and assignments as real-world-based as possible.

For example, in my composition courses, I not only allow students to choose their own essay topics, but I also encourage them to write about issues related to their prospective majors. I also assign readings (in addition to the old textbook standbys) from newspapers, popular magazines, even the Internet. Last semester I taught process writing using an essay from Yahoo! on improving credit scores.

We should also emphasize problem solving in our assignments and class activities. For research papers, I require students to identify a specific problem within the field they plan to enter and then explore various solutions. That's a very practical form of critical thinking.

Make the connection. Take advantage of every opportunity to connect what students are doing in class with what they will be doing some day as employees.

My students hear the term "the real world" so much that, by the middle of the term, they're starting to roll their eyes. But it's important for them to understand that the work we're doing now in class isn't just a series of meaningless exercises, another set of hoops for them to jump through on their way to a degree. They're going to have to do these things for real one day—describe processes, do research to find solutions, draw comparisons—and my course may be the last time anyone ever actually teaches them how.

I'm fortunate to bring a wealth of real-world experience to my teaching, as a copywriter, technical editor, and former midlevel manager. While I recognize that not all faculty members enjoy that same advantage, most should have some idea of what goes on in their fields outside of the classroom. If not, they can always import that experience by bringing in guest speakers or studying relevant essays or video clips.

As we link the knowledge and skills that we teach to the sorts of activities in which employees routinely engage, we will be providing our students with the very best kind of workforce development. In time, those students—tomorrow's taxpayers—may come to better understand the relevance of the liberal arts, as they see how our courses helped them reach their professional goals. One day they might even stop rolling their eyes.

Reflection questions for "The Liberal Arts Are Workforce Development":

1. What exactly is a "liberal arts" education?

_____

_____

_____

_____

_____

_____

_____

_____

2. What distinguishes such an education from "workforce development"?

_____

_____

_____

_____

_____

_____

_____

3. How does a liberal-arts education actually contribute to workforce development?

_____

_____

_____

_____

_____

_____

_____

_____

4. How can professors make connections for students between the things they're learning in class and the things they'll have to do one day as members of the workforce?

_____

_____

_____

_____

_____

_____

_____

_____

Welcome to My Classroom: ESSAYS ON THE FIRST YEAR OF COLLEGE

15

Cross-Training for the Brain

Most of us who teach core courses are used to having students in our classrooms who don't really want to be there. A common refrain we hear is, "I'm a (fill-in-the-blank) major. Why do I have to take (English, history, algebra, etc.)?"

On some level, I sympathize. I clearly remember, as an English major, wondering why I had to take biology. Now I understand, of course, but back then I didn't, so I don't really expect today's students to be any different. At the same time, it's no fun being told, essentially, that your life's work is useless. Especially when we know it isn't.

A few years ago, it got to the point where students in my literature survey courses were expressing the "why am I here?" sentiment so often and so openly—through body language, if nothing else—that I decided to start confronting it in my opening-day remarks.

I began with a metaphor that I thought many students could relate to—physical fitness, specifically muscle-building. I reminded them that the way people build muscle is by pushing against resistance, creating microscopic tears in the muscle fiber. Then new tissue forms to heal those tears, causing the muscle to grow larger. It's those microscopic tears that make us sore when we work out.

I then likened that process to the way our brains "grow" or expand as we push against intellectual resistance by grappling with difficult and unfamiliar concepts. And, just like our biceps, sometimes our brains get a little sore, too. But that is necessary in order to build increased thinking capacity, which is something all professionals need, regardless of their field.

My metaphor seemed to satisfy students until a couple of semesters ago, when one guy piped up and asked, "But why can't we just exercise our brains in our major courses? Don't we have to think in those, too?"

He had a point. Core courses in the liberal arts hardly have a monopoly on thinking skills. Students obviously have to use their brains in business, health science, and education courses, too. My weight-lifting metaphor was fine, as far as it went, but it was insufficient to illustrate the concept I was trying to get across.

Clearly, I needed a new metaphor.

I found one over the holiday break, when my twenty-something son came home to visit for a few days. A former high-school athlete, he's always been pretty fit, but when I saw him this time, I was impressed at how positively ripped he's become. So I asked him what he was doing for a workout these days, and he told me he'd gotten into CrossFit.

CrossFit, of course, is the brand name for a particular type of cross-training regimen, which fitness experts have long told us is the optimal form of workout. It involves doing different exercises on different days, working different parts of the body and different muscle groups. The result, for most people, is an unprecedented level of fitness. In addition, cross-training enables the individual to develop a wide range of athletic abilities—strength, speed, agility, quickness, endurance—in a way that no single set of exercises could do.

As I was preparing for the new semester, a few days after talking to my son about his workouts, it occurred to me that the reason my fitness metaphor had proved inadequate was that it was incomplete. The core curriculum is really a lot more like cross-training than like weight-lifting. Yes, to be mentally fit, we have to push against resistance. But we also must encounter different types of resistance and respond to them with different parts of our brain. That's why math majors need to study literature and English majors have to sit through math classes and all of them need to take history and science and fine arts, and so on.

What we have traditionally referred to as the "core curriculum" in reality is nothing more—or less—than cross-training for the brain.

Reflection questions for "Cross-Training for the Brain":

1. Why don't students really want to take classes that aren't part of their major?

    _____

    _____

    _____

    _____

    _____

    _____

    _____

    _____

2. How is developing thinking skills like weight-lifting? How is that metaphor insufficient?

    _____

    _____

    _____

    _____

    _____

    _____

    _____

    _____

3. What are the benefits of cross-training for an athlete?

_____

_____

_____

_____

_____

_____

_____

4. What does it mean to "cross-train" mentally, and what are the benefits to the student?

_____

_____

_____

_____

_____

_____

_____

16

The Four Properties of Powerful Teachers

American higher education seems to be experiencing a kind of teaching renaissance. Articles on the subject proliferate in *The Chronicle of Higher Education* and other professional publications, suggesting a renewed interest and commitment to the subject across academe.

As a faculty member for more than thirty years, I have been inspired and motivated by all the online chatter. It's made me think about the great teachers I've known—and I've known many, from kindergarten through graduate school and beyond. Several taught in my department when I served as chair, and I had the pleasure of observing them at work.

Those experiences have led me to conclude that, when we boil down all the metrics, we're left with four qualities that all powerful teachers possess. I'm not just talking about adequate, effective, or even good teachers. I'm talking about the ones who most move us, who have made the most difference in our lives, and whom we most wish to emulate. Perhaps we can't all be that kind of teacher, but I suspect many of us at least aspire to be.

So what makes those teachers so great?

Personality. Nearly all the great teachers I've watched in action have similar personality traits. To some degree, teaching is an ability, and just like musical or athletic ability, some people seem to have more of it than others. At the same time, just because you'll never play the Hollywood Bowl doesn't mean you can't do wedding gigs with your garage band. If you weren't born with the personality traits of a great teacher, you can still work to develop some of those traits.

Just what are those traits? Here are some I've identified, and you could probably add to this list: Great teachers tend to be good-natured and approachable, as opposed to sour or foreboding; professional without being aloof; funny (even if they're not stand-up comedians), perhaps because they don't take themselves or their subject matter too seriously; demanding without being unkind; comfortable in their own skin (without being in love with the sound of their own voices); natural (they make teaching look easy even though we all know it isn't); and tremendously creative, and always willing to entertain new ideas or try new things, sometimes even on the fly.

If none of these traits describe you, and you're afraid that means you'll never be a great teacher—well, maybe you're right. Or, you can work to develop some of those traits and become a much better teacher than you are now. And if you're fortunate enough to possess several of those traits already—as I suspect is the case with many who choose this profession—then you can still work hard to fine-tune those qualities.

Presence. What I mean by presence, in part, is the unmistakable capacity some people have to "own" any room. We might call it charisma, but it's more than that. It's the ability to appear completely at ease, even in command, despite being the focal point of dozens (or even hundreds) of people. To some extent, this aspect of presence is something you're either born with or not, although I would also argue that owning the room is an ability people can develop over time.

But that isn't the only relevant meaning of the word "presence" in the context of great teaching. In his recent essay, "Waiting for Us to Notice Them," *Chronicle* columnist and college professor James Lang talked about what he called "a pedagogy of presence." He argued that, just as we are sometimes disengaged in our interpersonal relationships, so, too, can we become disengaged in the classroom—simply going through the motions and barely acknowledging students at all.

© dotshock/Shutterstock.com

Yet the best teachers, as Lang concluded, are always "present"—fully in the moment, connecting with both their subject matter and their students. That's a type of presence to which we can all aspire, whether or not we're born with great charisma. All it takes is a degree of self-awareness, a little concentration, and a fair amount of determination.

Preparation. Speaking of determination, something else all teachers can do, regardless of their natural gifts, is prepare meticulously. Knowing what you're talking about can compensate for a number of other deficiencies, such as wearing mismatched socks, telling lame jokes, or not having an Instagram account. Preparation occurs on three levels: long term, medium term, and short term.

You, like most faculty members, have already accomplished the necessary long-term preparation by virtue of advanced degrees. That preparation will serve you well, and be your primary source of authority, from your first day in the classroom until your last.

In between, you must continue your education on a regular basis—by reading extensively in your field, attending conferences and seminars, conducting and presenting your own research, and remaining a practitioner of your art or science. You must also continue to learn and grow as a teacher by exploring new advances in pedagogy and technology that can help you in the classroom.

And in the short term, to be a powerful teacher you must go into every single class meeting as prepared as you can be, given the time you have. That means more than just reviewing your notes or PowerPoint slides. It involves constantly reassessing what you do in the classroom, abandoning those strategies that haven't proved effective, or are just outdated, and trying new ones. It means being so familiar with your subject matter that you can talk about it off the cuff.

Some of that will come with time, as your level of familiarity with your subject will naturally increase the more you teach it. Then again, just because you've been teaching a course for fifteen to twenty years doesn't mean you shouldn't approach it each term as if for the first time. It's that level of preparation that allows great teachers to make it all look so easy.

Passion. Of all the qualities that characterize great teachers, passion is the most important, by far. The Beatles famously sang, "All you need is love," and while in teaching that might not be entirely accurate, it is true that a little passion goes a long way. Or as St. Peter put it, love certainly "covers a multitude of sins."

Passion, or love, manifests itself in the classroom in two ways: love for students and love for your subject matter.

I'm always amazed, and more than a little puzzled, at how many of my colleagues don't seem to like students very much. Those faculty members are the ones who always buttonhole you in the hallway to talk about how irresponsible and disrespectful their students are; who take great delight in pointing out students' deficiencies or constantly regale you with examples of (supposedly) stupid things students have said or done; who are always tsk-tsking about "kids today."

I sometimes want to say, "If you dislike students so much, why are you in this business? Why in the world would you want to spend so much of your time with a bunch of people you find so disagreeable?"

Don't think, by the way, that students don't pick up on the disdain. They absolutely do. And my experience with evaluating faculty members over the years suggests that the teachers who are most widely disliked are the ones who most dislike students. Conversely, the faculty members who seem to love teaching and love (or at least really like) students are the ones who are the most popular and, I believe, the most effective.

You also have to love your subject matter. Students might not even like a course at first, especially if it's one they're required to take, but a teacher's passion for the subject can be extremely infectious.

Love of your field is probably a reason you became a teacher. But it may be that, after teaching the same thing year after year, you're beginning to get a little burned out. That's where preparation comes in. Perhaps becoming re-engaged with your field is just the spark your teaching needs to reignite the passion. Or maybe it's time to switch things up—bring in new reading assignments, try out some new technology, add a new in-class activity.

The point is that teaching is, in a way, like a relationship. You have to work hard sometimes to keep the passion alive, and yet it's vital that you do so. And if you don't, students pick up on that, too. If what you're covering in class every day seems to bore you, how do you expect them to be interested?

Maybe teaching just comes naturally to you. But even if it doesn't, you can still have a powerful impact on students. By learning what great teachers do and how they do it, and then applying those lessons in your own classroom, you could become one of the "greats," too. With apologies to Lady Gaga, your students will never know if you were born that way or not.

Reflection questions for "The Four Properties of Powerful Teachers":

1. What does it mean that higher education is experiencing a "teaching renaissance"?

_____

_____

_____

_____

_____

_____

_____

_____

2. What are some of the personality characteristics that great teachers seem to possess?

_____

_____

_____

_____

_____

_____

_____

_____

3. "Presence," in the context, can mean two different things. What are they, and how do they relate to teaching?

_____

_____

_____

_____

_____

_____

_____

4. What types of "love" must a good teacher have? Why is each of them important?

_____

_____

_____

_____

_____

_____

_____

17

Remembering My Best Teachers

Consider this a follow-up to, and an expansion of, my recent essay in *The Chronicle of Higher Education*, "The Four Properties of Powerful Teachers," which has been widely referenced, including in an October 2015 article for *The Journal of Dental Education* by Dr. Nadeem Karimbux.

One of my favorite parts of that essay actually ended up on the cutting-room floor—but purely for space reasons. I only get so many words, and I confess I exceeded that limit by several hundred. Rather than omit other parts she thought were more important, my editor chose to summarize a long passage with a few sentences—and I don't necessarily disagree with her decision. However, I believe the concepts I wrote about are definitely worth considering, so I'm happy to have this opportunity to revisit them here.

The passage in question appeared early in the essay, under the subheading "Personality." Recognizing that everyone is different, and that personality traits aren't necessarily something we can fully control, I was nevertheless attempting to identify key traits that most of my best teachers had in common, from kindergarten through graduate school. Note that when I say "my best teachers," I'm not just talking about the ones I liked the best, although that is generally true, as well. But what I'm really talking about are the teachers who made the greatest impact on me, who I most remember to this day—even though, in some cases, it's been more than forty years since I sat in their classroom—and whom I have most tried to emulate in my own teaching.

Perhaps you will recognize some of these traits as being present in your own favorite teachers.

They tend to be good natured and approachable, as opposed to sour or foreboding. Grouchy, short-tempered, misanthropic curmudgeons can sometimes make effective teachers, too, if for no other reason than that they prepare us for grouchy, short-tempered, misanthropic bosses. I had some of those teachers myself, especially in graduate school, and learning to cope with them was a valuable learning experience I would not wish to deny anyone. But most of my very best teachers were pretty easy to get along with—at least as long as I paid attention in class and did my work.

They're professional without being aloof. Most teachers tend to keep students at arm's length, the obvious message being, "I'm your teacher, not your friend." And that isn't a bad thing. Clearly, professionalism requires a certain amount of boundary setting, which can be difficult—especially when dealing with older students, where the age gap is often not all that wide and they might actually be your friends under different circumstances. My best teachers always seemed to somehow walk the very fine line between being an authority figure and someone I felt I could talk to—and generally speaking, they appeared to do it effortlessly. I didn't even understand what they were doing until years later, when I had to do it myself.

They have a good sense of humor (even if they're not stand-up comedians), perhaps because they don't take themselves or their subject matter too seriously. Few things are more off-putting to students than teachers who obviously think they're much smarter than anyone else in the room, perhaps in any room—unless it's teachers who think their subject is the most important subject of all and expect students to feel the same way and devote their time accordingly, other classes be darned. Such teachers rarely have a sense of humor when it comes to themselves, much less their subject matter. But my best teachers not only understood that their class was just one of several we were taking, but almost all of them had a great, self-deprecating wit, which they didn't hesitate to turn against themselves and even their topics.

They seem to enjoy what they do and enjoy being around students. I wrote in my *Chronicle* column about teachers who don't really like students—and I've been around a lot of them over the years. They're the ones who are constantly complaining about how rude or unprepared their students are, not to mention whining about their workload. I've often wondered: Why are those people even in this profession? What did they expect? The people I remember as my best teachers were the ones who clearly loved teaching and got a kick out of associating with students every day. After all, no one wants to feel like a nuisance, which is exactly how some teachers make their students feel. The best teachers don't.

They're demanding without being unkind. Some teachers I know take great pride in being disliked by students, wearing their unpopularity like a badge of honor. They naturally assume it's because they're so "demanding" and "rigorous"; since all those lazy students dislike rigor, they naturally transfer that dislike to the people who demand it of them. In my experience, however, most students want to be challenged; they don't mind if a lot is expected of them. They just don't want their teachers to be jerks or insufferable know-it-alls. I believe you can be as demanding as you want, within reason, without being mean-spirited. That's how my best teachers were.

They seem comfortable in their own skin. Perhaps one reason students tend to like these teachers is that they like themselves, without being in love with the sound of their own voice. This is related to what I said about the best teachers not taking themselves too seriously, but it goes beyond that. In my opinion, the root cause of bad teaching is a fundamental lack of self-confidence, leading teachers to overcompensate by being unreasonably demanding, aloof, and condescending to students. Paradoxically, the teachers who seem most arrogant and narcissistic are often trying to cover up what they perceive as profound deficiencies in their own personalities and abilities. The best teachers are confident without being arrogant, authoritative without being condescending.

They are tremendously creative, always willing to entertain new ideas or try new things—sometimes even on the fly. "Innovation" is a popular buzzword these days, to the point where simply being "innovative" has become desirable for its own sake, regardless of whether the resulting "innovations" actually accomplish anything worthwhile. The term is usually applied to technology, as if that were the only acceptable or significant type of innovation. My best teachers, though, were truly innovative, coming up with creative ways—as I said, sometimes spur of the moment—to help us students understand, internalize, and remember what they were trying to teach us. Sometimes those ideas involved what we commonly refer to as "technology"—meaning computers—but often they were very low-tech ideas. What made those teachers innovative was not their tools but their minds.

They make teaching look easy (even though we all know it isn't). Ultimately, great teachers are like great athletes or dancers or musicians. We may know, cognitively, that what they do isn't easy, but they consistently do it with so little apparent effort that we're often lulled into thinking it's no big deal—until we try it ourselves. Then we learn quickly just how difficult it is to play a sport or an instrument—or teach—at a very high level. In my case, even though I liked most of the teachers on my best-ever list, and actually loved some of them, I didn't really come to appreciate them and what they did until I became a teacher myself. Now I strive to emulate them and all too often fall short.

In closing, I'd like to acknowledge once again that the personality traits listed here are just that—personality traits–meaning we as individuals don't necessarily control whether or not we have them, or to what degree. No doubt, there's some truth to the idea that certain people are just born teachers, because they happen to be blessed with these traits in abundance.

At the same time, I do believe that, even if we're not necessarily born with all these traits, we can work to develop them and to some degree succeed. We may never be as funny or approachable or creative as our favorite teachers, or as we'd like to be. But simply by recognizing those as desirable traits that we wish to acquire, by acknowledging that we don't possess them to the degree we would like, and by committing ourselves to working on those areas, we can become more approachable, more creative—yes, even funnier—than we were before or would be otherwise.

To the extent that we undertake that journey of self-discovery and self-improvement, we become better teachers every day—whether we're "born teachers" or not.

Reflection questions for "Remembering My Best Teachers":

1. In what way is this essay a follow-up to "The Four Properties of Powerful Teachers"?

_____

_____

_____

_____

_____

_____

_____

2. Why is it so important for teachers to be approachable?

_____

_____

_____

_____

_____

_____

_____

3. Is it important for teachers to have a sense of humor? Why or why not?

_____

_____

_____

_____

_____

_____

_____

4. What exactly is the "journey of self-discovery and self-improvement" mentioned at the end of the essay?

_____

_____

_____

_____

_____

_____

_____

The Seven Fundamental Conditions of Learning

In "The Four Properties of Powerful Teachers" and "Remembering My Best Teachers," I wrote about the attributes of the **great teachers**, with the goal of identifying for young faculty members, in particular, the qualities they ought to emulate and cultivate. Several readers complained that my focus was too much on the teacher and not enough on students.

Fair enough. In this essay, I'll try to answer two questions: What do students need in order to learn? And how can we as teachers provide those things?

For the record, my aim here is not to rewrite **Bloom's taxonomy**, (mis)appropriate portions of it, or step on its toes. For its purpose—identifying the different ways in which students learn—the taxonomy cannot really be improved upon. I'm trying to do something different: Establish the fundamental conditions that must exist if people are to learn, drawing on my five decades as a student, teacher, and parent. I've come up with seven conditions.

1. Awareness. I'm sure it sounds self-evident to say that students, in order to learn, need some awareness of the subject matter at hand. That is, they must recognize that there is something they *need* to learn before they can hope to learn it. It's always sobering to realize just how many students not only don't know anything about the subject but don't even recognize how much they have to learn. They don't know what they don't know.

I've always believed that my first job, as a teacher, is to open students' eyes to the fact that there's a lot they don't know—a whole world of information out there in general, and about my subject in particular—that might ultimately be of use to them.

2. Interest. After establishing that there is much to learn, teachers must then answer the question of why students should care. That's a hard one, especially for those of us who teach general education or «core» courses, because most of our students are not naturally interested in what we're talking about. They're taking our class only because it's required for graduation or transfer and, frankly, would not darken our door otherwise.

That's why it's up to us, early on and often, to help them understand why the information we're sharing is meaningful to them personally. Otherwise, they're unlikely to feel very motivated and almost certainly will not learn as much as they could.

3. Motivation. Although experience suggests that students are more likely to learn if they have some interest in the subject matter, there are plenty of other reasons for them to pursue mastery—even if they don't care about the material or envision using it in the future. One good reason is grades and everything that goes with them: good academic standing; approbation from parents, peers, and others; and admission to an academic major or graduate program. I spent hours struggling with precalculus, not because I cared about math but because it was required and I didn't want to ruin my GPA.

Besides grades, one of the best forms of motivation I've found involves professional standards and expectations. Most students in my first-year composition courses have little interest in grammar or sentence structure as such, but their ears perk up when I explain that they're going to be judged in the workforce based on how well they use the language. Which brings me to the importance of relevance.

4. Relevance. Students learn more efficiently and effectively if they understand the relevance of a topic to anything else in their lives or the world at large. One of the biggest complaints about a college education—especially now, when even some bright students are considering skipping college altogether—is that it's largely theoretical. It's also true that a fair amount of theory is often necessary for students to fully grasp certain concepts.

But our courses don't have to be all theory. We should constantly be looking for opportunities to connect what we're teaching to the "real world" outside our classrooms (which includes, by the way, the rest of the college experience). I don't just mean bringing in news articles on current events or pop-culture references. I also mean showing students how the work they're doing in class will prepare them for what they'll be doing in a year or five years.

I tell my composition students from Day One to ignore the "ENGL" prefix. It's not an "English" or "language arts" course. It's a writing course, and the reason they're in it is that they're going to have to write their butts off just to get through college. And then they will spend the rest of their professional lives writing reports, proposals, letters, emails, and more. (They generally do not regard that as good news, but at least it makes the material immediately relevant.)

5. Engagement. Students who understand the relevance of what they're learning are more likely to become engaged with it. Engagement itself is something else they need in order to achieve mastery.

Of course, "engagement" has become kind of a buzzword, used to describe everything from flipped classrooms to service learning. But what does it really mean? For me, it means that students are immersing themselves in the subject matter. They're listening carefully in class, participating in discussions, and reading the text and other course materials closely. It also means they're thinking carefully about the concepts, especially those they find difficult.

Welcome to My Classroom: ESSAYS ON THE FIRST YEAR OF COLLEGE

© wavebreakmedia/Shutterstock.com

Most of all, engagement means that they have gone beyond mere listening and thinking to actually doing. That's easier in some disciplines than others. After all, students have to write in a writing class or conduct experiments in a biology lab. Getting students to "do" history or sociology might be more of a challenge, but I'm sure the best teachers in those disciplines have figured out how.

6. Reinforcement. That includes the repetition that is so necessary for learning, covering concepts again and again to make sure students understand. It also includes assessment, determining how well they are grasping concepts and then modifying our teaching accordingly. And it entails the motivational tactics (positive or negative) that teachers employ, such as grades, recognition, praise, constructive criticism, and so forth.

Mostly, though, I think of reinforcement in terms of students' desire to see evidence—apart from anything we or their textbooks say—that the material is actually important in the broader scheme of things. This is where bringing in articles, surveys, or even guest speakers can be valuable.

I cut my instructional teeth teaching technical writing to mostly upper-division engineering students. Talk about a bunch of folks who really didn't want to be there. Their body language practically screamed: "Why do we have to take another English class? We're engineers, for crying out loud."

After combating that level of resistance for a semester, I started bringing in, during the first week, an engineer friend of mine who had graduated from the same program. As he explained to them how much writing he had to do on a daily basis on the job, you could see their attitudes starting to change. That was some serious reinforcement.

7. Support. As college professors, we have a natural aversion to «hand-holding.» Yet sometimes a bit of hand-holding is precisely what the situation calls for—in the case of a terrified nontraditional student, for example, or a thoroughly lost first-generation student. Occasionally, we have to step out of our own comfort zones and expand our role from mere teacher to coach, counselor, or even cheerleader.

Support can take many other forms, too. It can mean making sure students have all the tools they need to succeed in the course. That includes intellectual tools (like critical-thinking skills), technical ones (mathematical formulae, organizational structures, or taxonomies), and physical resources (lab equipment, texts, and other course materials).

But primarily, we as faculty members have to build an environment in which students feel safe yet challenged, accepted yet pushed, valued as human beings yet evaluated as scholars. Our continuing quest, both individually and as a faculty, is not so much to figure out how to teach best as to figure out how to create a place where students can and will learn.

That is the quest of a career, of a lifetime, full or trial and error, fits and starts, failures and successes. But undertaking that quest is, for me, what it means to be a teacher, and it is worth every moment of time and every ounce of effort.

Reflection questions for "The Seven Fundamental Conditions of Learning":

1. Research Bloom's taxonomy. What is it, and what does it have to do with teaching and learning?

_____

_____

_____

_____

_____

_____

_____

2. What does it mean to say that "many students don't know what they don't know"? Can you think of any examples?

_____

_____

_____

_____

_____

_____

_____

3. What is the relationship, for students, between relevance of subject matter and motivation to learn?

_____

_____

_____

_____

_____

_____

_____

4. Where the student/professor relationship is concerned, what is the difference between "hand-holding" and support?

_____

_____

_____

_____

_____

_____

_____

Welcome to My Classroom: ESSAYS ON THE FIRST YEAR OF COLLEGE

19

Retention in the Trenches

Anyone who has worked at a community college or other access institution for more than a few years knows that the current emphasis on "college completion" is really just a repackaging of an age-old concern: retention. Essentially, the question before us is: How do we keep students in our classrooms and on our campuses long enough for them to either transfer or earn a credential?

That's a question access institutions have been asking for decades. What's changed lately is that many states are now factoring retention—or "completion rates"—into their funding formulas, which raises the stakes for colleges even higher.

Solutions to the retention dilemma have been both varied and recurrent—meaning that, over the past thirty years or so, we've not only tried a lot of different programs and gimmicks to keep students on track but have recycled many of them. I've lost count, for instance, of the number of times the colleges where I've worked have switched from faculty-based student advising to using professional advisers—and then switched back. The result: Many seasoned faculty members are understandably dubious—not about retaining students but about the latest administrative retention scheme du jour.

Obviously, we haven't yet discovered the magic formula, or else we wouldn't still be talking about this problem, much less potentially losing money because of it.

The good news is that faculty members can take steps on their own that might actually have some impact. Studies show that one of the most important factors affecting students' persistence and success is the quality of their classroom experience, or what student-retention expert Sherry Miller Brown calls "academic integration." That's especially true for students who are most at risk of falling by the wayside, such as nontraditional students and those in developmental courses.

So what can you do, in your own classroom, to help?

Be a teacher, not a gatekeeper. When I first started teaching composition—as a part-time instructor at a large research university—the program director made it clear that my job was not really to teach writing but to determine which students could write well enough to succeed on the campus and "weed out" the rest. That's what I refer to as a "gatekeeper" mentality.

I never cared for that approach. I love the craft of writing, believe anyone smart enough to make it into college can learn to do it reasonably well, and get a charge out of seeing students progress as writers. In short, I want to teach, not guard the gate to some mythical land of the intellectual elite. That's why I was attracted to the mission of two-year colleges: meeting students where they are and helping them get to where they need to be.

I've found that if at-risk students perceive their professors as gatekeepers rather than teachers, those students are more likely to quit when things get tough. After all, what's the point? They're not going to make it anyway—or so they conclude. But they're much more likely to stick it out if they see their professors as partners in the learning process.

Be flexible. One of the keys to stemming student attrition is to have a modicum of flexibility. At open-access institutions, our students deal with such a wide array of challenges—problems with their personal lives, health, and finances—that we sometimes have to make allowances. It's either that or else watch the failure of students who, with a little understanding, could have succeeded.

Some might argue that those students shouldn't be in college to begin with, because they clearly "haven't made it a priority." I would disagree, but the point is moot. Those students are in our classes, whether we like it or not. And we have the same responsibility to them as to any other students.

This past semester, I had: a student whose father died suddenly of a heart attack; a student undergoing extensive tests to determine the cause of her excruciating migraines; one who was diagnosed with leukemia; one who was hospitalized for two weeks for an unknown ailment; and one who is going through a messy divorce. As of this writing, it looks like all of them will complete my course. They're all bright, determined young people (younger than me, at least), who I'm convinced will earn college degrees. I don't intend to let one difficult semester send them into an academic tailspin.

But don't be a pushover. We all know that some students will take advantage if the professor is too wishy-washy. Not every "crisis" is life threatening, and many aren't even crises at all. It's vital for professors to have guidelines for student performance and behavior in the classroom. It's equally vital to stick to those guidelines, unless there are extenuating circumstances.

Indeed, many of our most at-risk students crave structure. In some cases, that's why they're at-risk to begin with—because they've never had much structure in their lives, either at home or at school. They come to us expecting and needing clear boundaries, and if we don't provide them, that fact alone could be enough to send some of them reeling into academic limbo.

In other words, being too flexible can create just as many problems as being completely inflexible. Sometimes students just need a little understanding, and sometimes they need us to hold their feet to the fire. Erring too much in either direction could cause us to lose them.

Be accessible—and approachable. Most of us know it's important to be available to students. That's why we dither around at the front of the room for five minutes after class, waiting to see if any students need to talk. That's why we keep office hours and publish our office phone numbers and email addresses. That's why we check email at 10 p.m., after the kids have gone to bed.

But too few of us recognize the importance of being approachable. That may, in part, be a matter of personality. People who become college professors tend to be somewhat shy, even taciturn, which students can mistake for aloofness. It never occurs to us that we don't seem approachable. We know we're nice, empathetic people who just want to help. Can't students see that?

Not always. For many students, professors represent imposing and sometimes intimidating figures. We have to go out of our way to seem more human, perhaps by chatting occasionally with students in the hallway or before class, asking them not-too-probing questions about their lives and sharing not-too-intimate details of our own. Otherwise, however accessible we are, many students are unlikely to come up to us after class or swing by our office (although they might still email at 2 a.m.).

Make the material relevant. If there's anything we've learned from all the "student engagement" literature, it's that a bored student is a student at risk of failing. And nothing causes students to disengage faster than feeling like what they're studying has no connection or relevance to their lives or future. That's why we have to work so hard to demonstrate that what we're talking about is actually important in the bigger scheme of things—especially if we're teaching core courses that students are required to take.

In my composition classes, I constantly preach about the importance of writing. Every time I introduce a new strategy or approach, I explain how it relates to "real world" writing, illustrating my point with actual scenarios and relevant examples. My goal is not to entice them to love writing, as I do (that's not going to happen, in most cases), but rather to help them understand that (1) it's in their own best interests to learn to do it well, and (2) they can do it if they apply themselves.

Take some personal responsibility. This is the one I've struggled with the most. For much of my career, I felt that whether or not students succeeded in my classroom was mostly up to them. I provided the framework for learning, but if they chose not to attend or turn in their work, well, they're adults and that's their decision.

It's not that I didn't care if they succeeded. I just believed the onus was on them, not me.

I still believe that's mostly true. You can't force students to do something they absolutely don't want to do. And yet, over the last few years, I've begun to step outside my comfort zone and reach out to students who have multiple absences, who haven't turned in an assignment, or who clearly seem distracted in class (and not just by their cell phones).

The results have been remarkable. I've discovered that, in many of cases, these students really wanted to talk to me but were afraid, either because they thought they had screwed up beyond hope of redemption or they found me personally intimidating. (Apparently I still have some work to do in the approachability department.) Most have been tremendously relieved and grateful that I took the first step. And in most cases, they were able to complete the course. I wonder what would have happened if I hadn't reached out? I suspect many of those students would have dropped the course and maybe left college.

Not all such interventions end happily. Even if we try, we can't reach every student, and sometimes we don't try as hard as we should and sometimes they don't respond. But even my relatively modest efforts in this regard seem to be paying dividends: Just in the last four years, the completion rate in my courses has gone up nearly 15 percent.

Those students I've helped represent just a tiny percentage of the ones who somehow fall off our radar. And helping them complete a particular course doesn't guarantee that they'll finish college or get a degree.

But one point that is often overlooked, in all the rhetoric, is that in order for students to complete college, they first have to pass individual courses. The retention battle is won one student at a time, one course at a time. And that's something we as faculty members do have some control over, whatever the latest administrative scheme.

Reflection questions for "Retention in the Trenches":

1. In what way is the new "college completion" initiative just a repackaging of the old retention initiatives?

    _____

    _____

    _____

    _____

    _____

    _____

    _____

    _____

2. Why do faculty members grow frustrated or even jaded over the various schemes for increasing completion?

    _____

    _____

    _____

    _____

    _____

    _____

    _____

    _____

3. What, according to Sherry Miller Brown, is one of the most important factors in determining whether or not a student persists? Why is it so important?

_____

_____

_____

_____

_____

_____

_____

_____

4. What are some things professors can do to help their students persist and succeed?

_____

_____

_____

_____

_____

_____

_____

_____

The Power of Positive Regard

A few months ago, I tagged along with my wife, a middle-school teacher, to a workshop on classroom management presented by the Center for Teacher Effectiveness. The session focused on the center's "Time to Teach" approach—the idea being that the less time teachers have to spend dealing with disciplinary issues, the more time they'll have to cover important concepts.

Classroom management is a topic that has long interested me, so I was curious to hear what the presenters had to say and whether it would apply to me as a college instructor. Of course, much of what I heard was more applicable to K-12 teachers. But I was surprised to learn, over lunch, that I was far from the only college professor in attendance. I was also pleased to discover that the seminar offered several useful takeaways for us postsecondary folks on concepts that are just as important in teaching young adults (and older adults) as they are in teaching children.

Foremost among those concepts, and my favorite part of the entire presentation, was what our speakers referred to as "unconditional positive regard," a phrase borrowed from the psychologist Carl Rogers. They argued that effective teachers can learn a great deal from effective parents, who love their children unconditionally. That doesn't mean letting children get away with anything they want; far from it. It means those parents approach both teaching and discipline from a position of unconditional love, and their children understand that from the outset.

The presenters also weren't saying that teachers must love their students in the same way, or to the same degree, that parents love their children—only that you are generally more effective as a teacher if your students know, up front, that you care about them as individuals. As the late Madeline Hunter, a pioneering educator, famously put it, "Students don't care how much you know until they know how much you care."

Of course creating an atmosphere of positive regard is easier in a fourth-grade classroom of twenty-eight students, or even in a college writing classroom of twenty-four, than in a crowded lecture hall filled with five hundred students. For that reason, this column is aimed primarily at faculty members at community colleges and other teaching-focused institutions, which tend to have small class sizes. However, it might also apply to those who teach upper-division and graduate-level seminars—basically, anyone with a small enough class to get to know all their students by name.

There's no way I can capture all the good information covered in the workshop in one column, but here are a few key points.

Building trust and rapport. No doubt we all agree that establishing rapport with students is a good idea—if you can pull it off. But I think sometimes we fall into the trap of assuming rapport has to do with personality, as if only teachers who are charismatic or entertaining can really establish rapport with students.

That's not true. In a 2001 journal article, William Buskist and Bryan K. Saville defined rapport simply as "an alliance based on trust." Rapport, they wrote, "is a positive emotional connection among students, teacher, and subject matter that emerges from the manner in which the teacher constructs the learning environment."

Educational research shows teachers can build trust and rapport in commonsense ways, for example, by being available (posting and holding office hours); discreet (keeping sensitive information confidential); fair (treating all students equally, grading equitably, and avoiding favoritism); and benevolent (never doing anything to take advantage of students, make them lose face, or embarrass them). That last one is especially important for college faculty members.

The importance of building trust and rapport cannot be overstated. Numerous K-12 studies have shown that a strong teacher–student connection leads to higher academic achievement and fewer behavioral problems. I see no reason why that would not hold true for college classrooms, as well.

©Tyler Olson/Shutterstock.com

Welcome to My Classroom: ESSAYS ON THE FIRST YEAR OF COLLEGE

Getting to know students. Let's be honest: Many of us in higher education tend to be a bit stodgy—some by nature and some because we learned it from our professors. I fall into that category myself, at times. We also have very specific ideas about "professionalism" and can be quite meticulous in defining and maintaining clear boundaries between ourselves and our students.

Obviously, a certain amount of caution is necessary, if for no other reason than that we're adults dealing with other adults (technically, at least), and so the lines can indeed become a bit blurred. But if we're not careful, we can also use "maintaining professional distance" as an excuse for failing to relate to students in positive and beneficial ways. There may be a natural gulf between us, but that doesn't mean we can't occasionally reach across that gulf or respond to students when they reach out to us.

One simple way to bridge that divide is to learn students' names and then use them regularly in and out of class. That should go without saying, but I fear it's an area where many college teachers fall short, including myself. However, as I've made more of an effort to learn and use students' names, I've been amazed at how positively they respond.

Another highly effective strategy involves what the workshop presenters described as "non-contingent interactions." A "contingent interaction" is when what we say to students depends entirely on what they say to us: They greet us and we reply in kind; they ask a question and we answer. A student complains that an assignment is too difficult and I say, "Welcome to college." Those sorts of interactions are a normal part of teaching, taking place dozens of times a day. There's nothing wrong with any of them (OK, my third example might err on the side of snarky). But when all of your responses are contingent on something students have said, you're just doing the minimum required of you as a teacher and a human being.

A "non-contingent interaction" is proactive, not reactive. It's when you reach out to students first—just to ask how they're doing or to inquire about a problem you've noticed—because you care enough to do so. Maybe you can't do that with every student every day, but you should try it as often as possible. And not just with the friendly, talkative students. It's especially important to go out of your way to chat with students who are shy, withdrawn, or standoffish. That may help to draw those students out and will prevent you from appearing to have favorites. Your goal here is to help students feel recognized and valued as individuals.

Letting students get to know you. This is something many college faculty members struggle with—either because we don't want to cross any lines, we don't want to make the course all about us, or we just value our privacy. Those are all good reasons for proceeding carefully in your interactions with students.

But remember, back when you were in elementary school, the first time you ran into your teacher at the supermarket? Remember how shocked you were to realize that he or she was an actual human being who did the same things other human beings do, like buy groceries? That's a powerful epiphany. Chances are, you looked at that teacher a little differently afterward. You probably felt slightly more connected.

You may or may not run into your students in the supermarket. But there's no reason you can't make some kind of personal connection with them in class—just by using examples from your life to illustrate points in the material. Just don't go overboard.

I know that for some readers, these suggestions might seem a little too new-agey or touchy-feely. I myself am much closer to "curmudgeon" than "nurturer." But I had been moving in the nurturing direction—toward establishing better rapport with my students—even before I attended this seminar. That was partly for my students' sake, because I worry about losing them to the many distractions of twenty-first-century college life. But it was also for my sake, because I was beginning to feel stuck in a rut. I wanted teaching to be fun again, and I thought one way to do that might be to make learning more enjoyable for my students.

Above all, I wanted to create a learning environment like the one Buskist and Saville describe, where "student and teacher unite to achieve course goals." This seminar provided me with some useful tools for doing just that, tools that have worked remarkably well for me as I've started to apply them. Anecdotally, my students have become noticeably more engaged, and I've seen fewer behavior issues (such as chit-chat or texting during class). Maybe these strategies can have a similar effect in your classroom.

Reflection questions for "The Power of Positive Regard":

1. What might a college professor learn about teaching by attending a conference designed for K-12 teachers?

   _____

   _____

   _____

   _____

   _____

   _____

   _____

   _____

2. What are some of the things good teachers can learn from good parents?

   _____

   _____

   _____

   _____

   _____

   _____

   _____

   _____

3. What does "rapport" really mean, and how can teachers go about establishing it in their classes?

_____

_____

_____

_____

_____

_____

_____

4. What's the difference between contingent and non-contingent interactions between teachers and students? Why are the latter so important?

_____

_____

_____

_____

_____

_____

_____

Welcome to My Classroom: ESSAYS ON THE FIRST YEAR OF COLLEGE

21

Conquering Mountains of Essays

A philosopher friend once told me about a concept he called "work-work balance." As we progress in our careers, he explained, we should seek an acceptable equilibrium between tasks we enjoy and ones we don't, ultimately spending more time on the former and less on the latter. That sounded right to me, and I have endeavored over the years to do just that.

Unfortunately for those of us who teach multiple sections of writing-intensive courses, that balance can be difficult to achieve. As much as we enjoy teaching—and maybe even advising, class prep, and other aspects of our jobs—there's simply no escaping the part most of us don't enjoy, or at least enjoy less: grading all those essays. That daunting chore seems always to be hanging over our heads and can easily become all-consuming, if we let it.

I have simply resolved not to let it. Despite teaching at least four sections of first-year rhetoric and composition each semester, I refuse to let my work life, much less my entire life, be defined by this one potentially unpleasant task. And so, over the years, I have developed an approach to grading that I believe enables me to serve my students well, while at the same time maintaining a degree of sanity and actually enjoying my job.

In sharing this approach, I am breaking one of my Cardinal Rules for Surviving at an Access Institution: Don't tell anyone what you do, because someone will tell you that you can't do it. But what the heck. I'm more than thirty years in, tenured, and received my last promotion years ago. Some of my advice might sound like heresy to those faculty members who are perpetual martyrs for the cause. But if, like me, you have no interest in being a martyr—if you're tired of being haunted day and night by looming stacks of essays (actual or virtual) and would like to introduce a modicum of balance back into your life—here is my approach.

Change your bad attitude about grading. That's been a struggle for me, because I've always disliked it. However, over time I have come to understand that grading is not a task separate from teaching but rather an integral part of the teaching process. Marking students' essays offers me a chance to reinforce what I say in class and show students how those concepts actually play out on the page. At the same time, the issues I see in students' papers become fodder for useful classroom discussions.

As part of your attitude adjustment, stop complaining about how much grading you have to do. Avoid those hallway conversations where you and your colleagues try to one-up each other with tales of woe about lost weekends spent buried under a pile of essays. In fact, avoid those grumbling colleagues altogether. I'm afraid we've gotten to the point (in my discipline of composition, at least) where spending untold hours grading and then bemoaning that fact—loudly, to anyone who will listen—has become a perverse badge of honor. You can do without that kind of negativity.

Stagger due dates. Managing your grading load requires some advance planning. If you're getting four sets of essays at the end of the week, so you have to fight your way through the piles over the weekend, that's mostly your fault. There's no reason you can't construct your syllabi so that various classes—yes, even different sections of the same course—turn their essays in on different days.

That may require some creativity on your part, but the effort will seem well worth it when those essays don't arrive all at once. Remember: When they aren't submitted at the same time, they don't have to be returned at the same time.

Break it down. As most of us know from writing theses or dissertations, the key to completing any major project is to break it down into small, manageable segments. That's certainly true of grading.

My composition courses are typically capped at twenty-four students, so an easy breakdown for me is to grade twelve essays, or half a class, each day. In fact, I typically divide up the task even further, grading no more than six essays in one sitting. Then I'll go do something else for an hour before coming back to finish the other six. That breaks up the monotony and enables me to approach each set of six essays mentally fresh. We all know

© Kagai19927/Shutterstock.com

that when we try to read too many essays at once, they all start to run together. Sometimes we even judge common errors more harshly in papers at the bottom of the stack, just because we get tired of seeing them. That's not fair to those students.

Schedule grading time. It helps me to schedule my activities, especially those—like writing, exercise, and grading—I might otherwise prefer to avoid.

I can usually get all my grading done if I spend two hours a day, five days a week on it. As long as I stick to that schedule, I rarely have to grade on weekends or in the evenings. The catch, of course, is that I really do have to stick to my schedule, whether I want to or not.

When I say "schedule," I mean that literally. I look at my calendar each week, see where I have class times, office hours, and committee meetings blocked off, then find a couple of hours each day for grading and block those off, too. Once grading hours are on my schedule, I hold them sacrosanct, unless something major comes up (the latest cute cat video on Facebook is not something major).

Have a realistic return policy. At one end of the spectrum are instructors who stay up all night trying to give graded essays back to students the next day. At the other end are those who return every paper at the end of the semester. You don't want to be either of those people.

I've always believed I have a professional obligation to return students' essays within a reasonable amount of time, and certainly before the next essay is due. I've chosen to define "a reasonable amount of time" as one week, or two class sessions. Occasionally, if I get four stacks of papers in the same week, it might take me three class meetings to finish grading.

I put my commitment to my students in writing on my syllabus: If they turn their papers in on time, I will return them within two class meetings if possible, three at most. (If they turn their essays in late, I note, I'll get to them when I get to them. You might be surprised how that veiled threat cuts down on late essays.)

Be a teacher, not an editor. Something I've struggled with, having done a fair amount of copy editing in my time, is the temptation to edit students' essays, not just grade them—to mark through entire sentences and write over the top and make other wholesale changes to their writing.

I have to remind myself constantly that that's not my job. I'm not helping students prepare a manuscript for publication; I'm trying to help them improve their writing. Simply changing the way they've written something, in a way that might seem arbitrary to them, is usually not an effective means of accomplishing that. So I try to limit my "editing" to situations where a simple change of wording or construction might have broader application than to that one essay.

Eschewing editing also means I don't necessarily mark every single "error" I see. We can easily fall into the trap of giving students too much feedback, so that they can't possibly process it all. It's much better, I believe, to focus on two or three problems in a given paper, help the student overcome them, and then perhaps focus on different issues in the next assignment.

Limit your comments. The same rule applies to making comments at the end of students' papers. I have colleagues whose comments are longer than the essays themselves, although I've never seen any evidence that such a strategy is effective or that most students even read those long comments. (Most graduate students, maybe, but not most of my undergraduates.)

Instead, try offering a few salient observations that students can actually take to heart and learn from. If you've already commented on those issues in the margins you probably don't need to repeat yourself at the end.

At the end of each essay, I try to make at least one positive comment, followed by no more than three "suggestions for improvement."

Limit grading time on each essay. By grading instead of editing, by not marking every single error you see, and by limiting your comments to what students will actually read and find meaningful, you should be able to get through the typical 600- to 800-word essay in about ten minutes or less.

Let's be honest: If you've been doing this for any length of time, you probably know within two or three minutes approximately where a particular essay falls on the grading scale. All that's left is to fine-tune the grade (middle B or low B?), note any significant problems, and offer a few useful comments. You can sacrifice yourself further on the altar of "good teaching" if you insist, but there's really not much more you can do with that essay that's going to be of any genuine benefit to students.

So, to do the math: If I spend no more than ten minutes on each essay, that means I can grade twelve essays within two hours. In that manner, it will take me eight business days to get through four class sections of papers. If I've effectively staggered my due dates, I can return all of those papers within three class periods, at most.

And that's how you teach four sections of composition (or any other writing-intensive course) without being miserable all the time, burning yourself out, or losing your sanity. You might even enjoy your job, not to mention your life. Of course, if you prefer, you can just be miserable all the time, like too many of the people I know who teach composition. But I don't recommend it—and it won't make you a better teacher.

Reflection questions on "Conquering Mountains of Essays":

1. Why is it important for professors to find some balance in their lives—both "work-life" balance and "work-work" balance?

_____

_____

_____

_____

_____

_____

_____

2. What are the differences between being a teacher and being an editor, and why are those differences so important?

_____

_____

_____

_____

_____

_____

_____

3. What are some steps instructors can take to lessen the time they spend grading while still doing a good job?

_____

_____

_____

_____

_____

_____

_____

4. Why won't spending more time than necessary grading make you a better teacher?

_____

_____

_____

_____

_____

_____

_____

Literary Analysis as Scientific Method

For years I've tried to figure out how to get my "Introduction to Literature" students—99 percent of them not English majors—to appreciate literature. And by "appreciate," I don't mean "like." That's probably a lost cause. I just mean I want them to be able to understand what a writer is saying, how he or she goes about saying it, and what relevance it might have to their lives.

As anyone who has taught a course like that knows very well, this is an uphill battle. Or at least it was for me until a couple of years ago, when I had an epiphany. Two, actually. The first was that the thinking process I've been trying to get students to apply to literary texts is really not that different from what my undergraduate science professors referred to as the scientific method. The second was that, in our hyper-technological society, most students definitely see the relevance of science, even if they don't see the relevance of literature.

I hope I won't offend my science colleagues too much if I define the scientific method broadly here as consisting of three main steps: observe, hypothesize, and experiment. At least, that's what I was taught, or something very close to it. If I'm guilty of misstating or oversimplifying, perhaps I can be granted a certain amount of literary license. Those three steps are adequate for what I'm trying to accomplish.

I explain to my students that they can interpret a poem, for example, simply by applying the scientific method as I've just defined. And how, I ask them, do we "observe" a poem? "By reading it," someone is sure to answer. Exactly, I tell them, but it's not enough just to give it the once-over. A research psychologist doesn't just peek in on the rats occasionally and say, "Hey, look what they're doing now. How cute." No. The researcher spends hours, days, weeks observing the rats, thinking and asking questions about their behavior, taking copious notes.

So too when we read a text, we must read it multiple times, read it slowly and carefully, constantly asking ourselves, "What does this mean? What is the poet trying to say?" We must pay special attention to any particular words, passages, or elements (such as structure) that seem especially significant or perplexing and ask ourselves what they signify, how they fit in with the work as a whole.

As we read in this way, we begin over time to come up with a theory of what the poem might be about—in other words, a hypothesis. At this point it's just a hypothesis, nothing more. But at least it's a place to start.

The real work lies in experimenting, or testing the hypothesis. You might begin with, "I think, in 'Mending Wall,' Frost is trying to say that people put up walls whether they want to or not." Okay. That's a hypothesis. Now experiment. Start at the top and test your hypothesis against what the poem actually says: "Something there is that doesn't love a wall." Check. "We keep the wall between us as we go." Check. "Before I built a wall I'd ask to know / What I was walling in or walling out." Check. "He moves in darkness as it seems to me." Check.

In this case, my hypothesis works. That's not to say it's the definitive answer, but at least it's defensible. If it didn't work, if there was some point in the poem where I said to myself, "Nah, that doesn't make sense," then I'd have to go back, read some more, and formulate a new hypothesis. But when it does work, voilà! I have a paper topic.

In an essay, of course, the "hypo"-thesis becomes just the plain old thesis, and the elements or passages in the poem that fit the hypothesis become the pieces of supporting evidence that fill out the body paragraphs. That much seems to be pretty easy for students to understand.

Since I've been taking this approach, student engagement in my intro-to-lit classes has improved dramatically and so have their essays. They no longer seem to assume that literature is something they can't possibly understand, much less write about, and I give the scientific method all the credit for that.

At least, that's my hypothesis, and I'm sticking to it.

Reflection questions for "Literary Analysis as Scientific Method":

1. What does it mean for students to "appreciate" literature, in this context? What doesn't it mean?

2. What is the scientific method? How does it apply to analyzing literature?

3. At what point does a "hypothesis" become a thesis?

_____

_____

_____

_____

_____

_____

_____

4. Why are non-English majors likely to find this method of literary analysis more engaging than what they've been exposed to in the past?

_____

_____

_____

_____

_____

_____

_____

23

How I (Finally) Got
My Students to Read

Anyone who teaches literature knows how difficult it is to get students to read—especially in a sophomore-level survey course, which most students are taking only because it's required for graduation and in which virtually none of them have the least bit of personal interest.

So what do you do? Cajole? Threaten? I've tried both, with limited success. I tell students on Day One that the course will be much more interesting if they've read their assignments and we can discuss them together in class, rather than my just lecturing for the entire period. I also explain that they will be tested on the readings and, if they don't read, they can't hope to do well on the tests.

As I said, neither of those exhortations has been particularly effective. Students may find me boring, but apparently they'd rather listen to me drone on for seventy-five minutes than go to the trouble of reading the assignment. And sure enough, in a typical class, more than half bomb on the first test precisely because they didn't do the reading.

Sound familiar?

It's true that most of my students start reading (somewhat) after they see their first test grades because they don't want to bomb on the second one, too. But this past semester I decided that wasn't good enough. They were missing too much good stuff. I wanted to come up with a way of getting them to read early on, without begging or threatening.

Of course, something else all of us know who teach reading-heavy courses is that the most effective way to get students to read assignments is to give regular quizzes. But quizzes have their drawbacks, too. They seem high-schoolish. They take up a lot of class time. They create more paperwork for the instructor. Students hate them. (Oh, wait. That's not a drawback.)

After some thought, what I came up with is what I'll call the mini-quiz. Actually, it's one long quiz, given in small increments of one question a day. And not even every day. Over the course of the semester—thirty class meetings—I asked my students twenty questions about their reading assignments. They never knew on which days they were going to get a quiz question, and they rarely knew exactly what work that one question would cover. If they wanted to be prepared, they had to read the entire assignment.

I always tried to ask fairly obvious questions about surface features, not deep meaning. That way, anyone who had done the reading would be able to answer, even if he or she didn't fully understand the work. For example, I might ask, "At the beginning and end of the story, what was Young Goodman Brown's wife, Faith, wearing in her hair?" Anyone who has read the story, by Nathaniel Hawthorne, knows the answer to that question. It doesn't require analysis. But you probably wouldn't pick it up just by skimming right before class, either.

After asking the question and giving students sufficient time to answer, I then told them the answer and let them mark their own papers, on the honor system. I also had them answer the questions on a single sheet of paper that they were responsible for keeping track of and turning in at the end of the semester. At that point I totaled up and recorded the number of correct answers.

Did that method open the door for cheating? Probably, although I'm pleased to say that at the end of the semester, as I went through their quizzes, I saw very little evidence of cheating. The only students who got all twenty questions right were the same ones who made As on all the tests. Most claimed thirteen to seventeen correct answers, which seems about right. Several acknowledged that they had not gotten any correct or very few—and those admissions corresponded with the lowest grades in the class.

Even if they did cheat, the quiz was for extra credit, anyway. Students could receive up to 20 points of extra credit (1 point for each correct answer), to be added to their final total before I averaged. Between tests and papers, there are 500 possible points in my class; it takes 450 to get an A, 400 to get a B, and so on. So 20 is a significant number without being make-or-break. In other words, it's enough to prod them to read their assignments but probably not enough to risk wholesale cheating.

At least, that's what I thought going in, and that seems to have turned out to be the case. Based on their class participation, I concluded that more students had read their assignments than in past semesters. Our discussions were livelier, more inclusive, and more fun. Students' test grades (and final grades) were noticeably higher (even on the first test). The quizzes even helped with attendance and punctuality because I asked the quiz questions at the beginning of class and students weren't allowed to "make up" missed questions.

Over all, I was quite pleased with the "mini-quiz" strategy. I will probably tweak it somewhat for future semesters, but I plan on making it a central feature of my lit survey courses from now on.

So what was Faith wearing in her hair in the Hawthorne story? It was pink ribbons.

Reflection questions for
"How I (Finally) Got My Students to Read":

1. Why is it so important for students in a literature class to read their assignments? Why don't they want to read?

\
\
\
\
\
\
\
\

2. What are some of the problems with traditional quizzes? How do "mini-quizzes" address some of those problems?

\
\
\
\
\
\
\
\

3. How do these "mini-quizzes" motivate students to read?

_____

_____

_____

_____

_____

_____

_____

4. Why isn't cheating on these quizzes such a big issue?

_____

_____

_____

_____

_____

_____

_____

Of White Boards and PowerPoints

This semester I have two sections of the same composition course that meet back-to-back in the same room—a room with old white boards that don't erase very well. The other day I was writing on the board during the second of the two when a student noticed that I was tracing over the still-visible outlines of what I had written for the earlier class, and that it was basically the same thing.

"Why did you bother erasing?" he asked. "Why didn't you just leave it up there so you don't have to write it all over again?"

Why, indeed? For that matter, why don't I just put everything I would typically write on the board into a PowerPoint slide show, as so many of my colleagues have done? Then I'd never have to write it at all.

The answer, I think, is that first of all I like writing on the white board, instead of sitting behind a computer and scrolling through slides. Writing on the board is, if not interactive, at least active, something that gets me up and moving around. I tend to think better when I'm moving around. (I wrote most of this blog post in my head while taking a five-mile walk this afternoon.)

Moreover, even if I've written the same stuff on the board two other times that day, in two other classes, as far as the students are concerned I'm writing it just for them (unless they can still see the ghostly remains of last period's scribbles).

Finally, and most important, I'm not really writing the same stuff. It may be more or less the same, but it's not exactly the same. Every class period is different, and every group of students is different. I love to let them brainstorm aloud about papers we're working on while I write down their ideas on the board, and even though two classes may come up with some of the same ideas, they also hit upon different ones. For that matter, I sometimes see things differently, too, from one period to the next, as I'm stimulated by their suggestions.

Trying to capture all that in a PowerPoint presentation would destroy the spontaneity that I believe is a big part of the writing process, especially at the early stages. That's something I'm definitely attempting to model for them as I write on the board.

I am not, despite what you may have heard, a technophobe. I do use the data projector and pull-down screen pretty regularly to go over readings with students or show them examples of good and bad sentences or whatever. I sometimes even compose on the screen for them, walking them through it, so they can get a better feel for the drafting process. I can do that much more easily (and legibly) via computer than writing by hand. For those reasons and more, I love having a data projector in the room.

But for me, it won't ever fully replace the white board—especially if we're able to find the money to actually replace some of our white boards.

Reflection questions for "Of White Boards and PowerPoints":

1. What are some of the strengths and weaknesses of using PowerPoint presentations to teach a class?

_____

_____

_____

_____

_____

_____

_____

_____

2. What are the strengths and weaknesses of writing on the white board?

_____

_____

_____

_____

_____

_____

_____

_____

3. What does it mean to be "active, if not interactive"? How does being active benefit the teacher and enhance the classroom environment?

_____

_____

_____

_____

_____

_____

_____

4. Is preferring to write on the white board instead of using PowerPoint presentations a form of technophobia? Why or why not?

_____

_____

_____

_____

_____

_____

Resolving to Be Better (Rated)

The whole concept of New Year's resolutions has never appealed to me—perhaps because, as a teacher, I'm more inclined to think of the "new year" as beginning in August rather than January. Over the recent winter holiday break, however, I spent a fair amount of time pondering how I could improve my classroom performance, spurred to some degree by my student reviews on RateMyProfessors.com.

I know many faculty members don't place much credence in such informal, online evaluations. But I find them to be remarkably honest, as well as reasonably—sometimes piercingly—accurate. I'm also impressed that only those students who feel strongly about a particular course or professor, one way or the other, are likely to go to the trouble. Even if online ratings represent, to some degree, the extremes of student opinion—those who either really liked the class or really hated it—they still contain a great deal of useful information.

For that matter, much the same could be said these days of my college's more formal student evaluations. Like a lot of institutions, we moved a few years ago to a paperless system, meaning students receive an email in their college account (which you know they all check religiously) and then have to click on a link and log onto a website to fill out the form. Once again, only the most motivated students are likely to complete the process, which effectively means formal evaluations are now little different from the informal variety.

The bottom line: If I want meaningful feedback, I'm going to have to include RateMyProfessors in the mix. The days are long gone when we could hand out 25 copies of the evaluation form on the last day of class and realistically expect to get 22 of them back (remember having to deputize a student to collect the forms and deliver them to the department office?).

My overall ratings are pretty good; about 4.3 on the site's 5-point scale. But while it's certainly ego-enhancing to read some of the nice things students say about me, that sort of praise isn't particularly helpful (except, perhaps, to the extent that it lets me know what I'm doing right). It's the comments that sting a bit—and maybe more than just a bit—that tell me where I probably need to change.

For example, in the middle of an otherwise-favorable review, one student lobbed this little grenade: "He's often long-winded in his lectures." Lest I dismiss that as a one-off, throwaway line, the same sentiments were echoed in another student's less diplomatic pronouncement: "HE LOVES TO RAMBLE ON IRRELEVANT SUBJECTS. SO BORING!" (The caps here are the student's, not mine.)

"What?!" I thought to myself when I first read those reviews. "Me? Long-winded? Boring? I do not ramble. Well, maybe a little. Occasionally. OK, fine, I guess I can be a little long-winded at times."

The truth is, in my writing courses, I really don't "lecture" much. Most of the time, when I'm up in front of the class, we're supposed to be having a discussion—except that the students don't always discuss a topic as much as I would like. So, sure, it's kind of like a lecture. I get that. And I do occasionally bring examples or anecdotes into the discussion that aren't directly related to the topic at hand, although in my mind they're at least tangentially related and intended to illustrate some larger point.

But perhaps the connection isn't entirely clear to my students. And apparently I talk too much.

So I've resolved to take two steps to improve the classroom experience for my students. First, I'm going to make minor changes in the way I structure my syllabus. As I said, I don't lecture much in a writing class (or at least, I thought I didn't). We do plenty of other things—individual writing exercises, small group discussions, and so forth. But I've realized that I typically use most of a class period to introduce some new concept—in other words, I talk for the better part of an hour—and then devote the bulk of the next meeting to more interactive exploration of the concept.

Henceforth, I'm going to try to do a better job of mixing things up, giving fewer and shorter "lectures"—no more than 20 to 30 minutes of me talking—interspersed with active learning.

Second, as I've read articles in *The Chronicle* and elsewhere about how to foster better classroom discussions, I've come to realize that I've been taking the easy path of answering my own questions rather than encouraging and enabling students to shoulder more collective responsibility for the conversation. Beginning this semester, I intend to work a little harder to draw students out so that my "lecture/discussion" segments include more of the latter and less of the former.

Another complaint from some students (and this one really hits home) is that I talk too much about myself. Said one student, "He makes sure you don't forget how qualified he is." Another offered, "You can expect him to mention his publications."

"Do I really do that?" I wondered. And the answer is: "I guess I do, at least a little bit, mostly on the first day of the semester."

In my defense, my objective has been to establish some credibility early on. I'm trying to persuade students that I know what I'm talking about, because some of the things I'll be telling them about writing over the next several weeks will be very different from what they've heard in the past, particularly from their high-school teachers. My intention is not to brag about my accomplishments as a writer—which are relatively meager, in any case—but apparently that's the way it comes across to some students.

So in the future, I plan to tone down the "about me" part of my course introduction, keeping in mind the simple truth that the course really is not about me.

Some students complain in their ratings that it's too difficult to get an A in my courses. That's one thing I don't intend to change. Honestly, I didn't set out to be a "hard grader." I never give much thought one way or the other to where I fall on the easy-to-tough grading continuum. I'm just trying to help students improve their writing so they can succeed in college and beyond. While I'm convinced that most students can become proficient writers, if they put their minds to it, experience suggests that few of them will ever be excellent writers—hence the few A's in my writing courses.

For some students, that is unforgivable. As one exclaimed in obvious frustration, while giving me a poor review, "Professor Jenkins grades based on your performance!"

Oh, the horror.

However, I do give credence to a few reviews that made a related complaint: I'm not always as clear as I could be about my expectations. While I explain my grading standards and process early in the semester, I've never been a big fan of rubrics, which I find limiting and artificial. However, I see now that I probably need an actual document, something rubric-like that I can share with students to help them understand what's expected of them and how they will be evaluated.

As the new term begins, I'm hopeful that the time I spent reading through my RateMyProfessors reviews—as painful as it sometimes was—will in the long run improve my teaching.

Reflection questions for "Resolving to Be Better (Rated)":

1. Why should professors consider RateMyProfessors along with more formal evaluations?

_____

_____

_____

_____

_____

_____

_____

2. What is the value of bad reviews? Of good reviews?

_____

_____

_____

_____

_____

_____

_____

3. Why can it be problematic for professors to lecture too much in class?

_____

_____

_____

_____

_____

_____

_____

4. How can professors use their ratings or reviews to improve their teaching?

_____

_____

_____

_____

_____

_____

_____

Writing with a Heavy Teaching Load

A recent essay by Rachel Toor, "The Habits of Highly Productive Writers," clearly resonated with readers, and it's easy to see why: It contains practical information for academics seeking to boost their written output, and approaches the topic in a way that, for me, makes the whole endeavor seem a bit less daunting. I can imagine many readers came away from her piece thinking, "I can do this."

And yet, I can also imagine that a lot of full-time faculty members at community colleges and other teaching-focused institutions found themselves also thinking, "That would be nice—if only I had the time to write."

I'd like to follow up Rachel's excellent advice with an encouraging word of my own, aimed specifically at faculty members who, like me, have a heavy teaching load: You CAN find time to write, if that's what you really want to do. It won't be easy, but there are ways to manage a heavy teaching (and service) load and still write and publish more than you're doing now.

I usually teach five courses every semester. And since my discipline is writing, that means a lot of grading. I also advise students, serve on a couple of committees, (mostly) attend the required meetings, staff the department booth at campus open houses—all the same things done by most faculty members at teaching-focused colleges. In addition, I have a family and a moderately active social life.

Despite all that, this past fall semester (just as an example), I wrote a weekly column for a local newspaper, along with my monthly installments of The Two-Year Track for *The Chronicle* and periodic blog posts for *Vitae*. In addition, I published several essays in other venues, finished the last three chapters of my third book, and submitted a proposal for Book No. 4. I also cut a jazz album, learned to speak Mandarin Chinese, and built a life-size replica of the Millennium Falcon out of Legos.

OK, I made up those last three. But I did write well over 50,000 words this past semester. I don't say that to brag. On the contrary, my message is that if I can do it, so can you. I am not, by nature, an exceptionally hard-working or organized person. Like a lot of you, I suspect, I'd much rather be curled up somewhere with a good book.

But I decided several years ago that I was going to write, and so I started writing—and kept at it. You can do the same, even with a heavy teaching load, by following a few simple pieces of advice:

Commit. The first step—as with most other worthwhile things in life—is to decide that you really want to write and that you're willing to make certain sacrifices to achieve that goal. Because the key to writing, just like exercise or dieting, is to (with apologies to Nike) just do it.

I've lost count of the number of colleagues who have said they would like to write a book—"someday" when they "have more time." One thing we learn as we age, though, is that there's never going to be some magical point in the future when we suddenly find ourselves with an overabundance of spare time. On the contrary, as I've gotten older, life has gotten more complicated, not less.

If you want to write, you might as well start now. It's not going to get any easier. Ten years from now, you can either still be saying that you'd like to start writing someday or you can be counting your publications.

Organize and prioritize. The next step is to arrange your life so that you can make time for writing. I'm not talking about scheduling your writing time (we'll get to that in a moment). Before you even reach that point, you have to make sure you're not letting other important things fall through the cracks.

Obviously, that includes teaching and its attendant responsibilities, such as grading and course prep. You can't afford to let those duties slide at a teaching-oriented college, or else you might find yourself with more writing time on your hands than you wanted.

At the same time, certain mundane, familiar tasks can take over your life if you let them. So don't let them. In addition to classes, office hours, and meetings, which are already scheduled, you also need to set aside specific times for grading, class prep, and so forth. Then keep to that schedule as closely as possible.

That may require some sacrifices or changes in your priorities. Remember I said that I serve on a couple of committees? Well, I used to serve on four or five, but I've scaled back in order to free up more time for writing. Of course, that's easier to do for someone like me, who already has tenure and a fair amount of seniority, than it might be for people early in their careers. But to find time to write, you will undoubtedly have to jettison some other activities, as you're able. (Some new faculty members take on far too much anyway; learning to say no sometimes is advantageous.)

This advice applies to your personal life, as well. If you're like me, you don't want to take any more time away from your family than necessary—but you may have to steal a few hours here and there if you want to write. Perhaps you can get up a little earlier in the morning. Maybe you can come home from the office a little later some days. Maybe you can find an hour or two on Saturday or Sunday morning while others in your household are still asleep. Again, you're going to have to make some sacrifices, and family time and "me time" might be among them.

Schedule. There are two things in my life that I need to do but absolutely will not do unless I schedule them: exercise and writing.

Note that when I say "schedule," I mean that literally. I look at my calendar each week, with my classes, meetings, family commitments, etc., and block out segments of time when I'm going to write. (Just as I block out segments for exercise.) Three or four times a week, I try to set aside two-hour blocks of time to write. I know many experts say that you should write every day, and I don't necessarily disagree. There are just some days when I don't have any time to write—at all. But I've found that if I schedule blocks of time for writing, and hold them sacrosanct, I can generally use them productively.

That last sentence is key. Once you have looked at your calendar and scheduled time to write, that time must become inviolable, with the exception of family emergencies. (Your daughter forgetting her soccer cleats isn't an emergency. She can wear her trainers or borrow a friend's old pair for one day.)

As we all know, as soon as you sit down to write, it seems like dozens of things are suddenly competing for your attention, including Facebook and your cell phone. Those things can wait. For now, it's time to write, so get to it.

If it helps, find a special place to write where you will face a minimum of distractions. I confess: I do a lot of my writing at McDonald's. It has just the right ratio (for me) of peace-and-quiet to background noise. No one bothers me there, and Wi-Fi is available if I need it but too inconvenient to be a constant distraction. And, yes, I know I shouldn't, but I like the fries.

Be patient. At first, writing in increments, in those relatively short blocks of time that you've set aside, may seem painfully slow. You might feel like you're not getting anywhere, especially if you're working on a book. Just be patient. Over time, you will be surprised at how quickly the pages stack up. The important thing, as many of you no doubt learned from writing a dissertation, is to be consistent.

When I wrote my first book, my schedule was such that I could devote only one hour a day to the project. So I did. I wrote from 2 p.m. to 3 p.m., Monday through Friday. On many days, it seemed like I wasn't accomplishing much, producing only a couple hundred words, if that. On other days the writing flowed a little better and I might produce 1,000 words or more. But after 10 months of holding myself rigorously to that schedule, I had a 300-page manuscript, which I spent another four or five months revising.

Repurpose. A concept that all professional writers understand is that of repurposing, or reusing, things you've already written. That is especially important when you're writing incrementally. Blog posts can be expanded into columns and columns into articles. Articles can become book chapters, and vice versa. A scholarly piece, revised and condensed, can make an excellent general-interest column for the local newspaper.

The point is to increase your output without unnecessarily duplicating your effort. Writers who publish a lot are constantly looking for such opportunities. In fact, I learned about repurposing from my dad, a professional writer and photographer for four decades. To promote his first book of photographs, back in the early 1990s, he wrote three versions of essentially the same article for three different national magazines.

So contrary to what you may have thought, you really do have time to write—you've just been using that time for other things. But if you're willing to rearrange your work and personal life, make some sacrifices, and be patient, you can become a published and perhaps prolific author, even while teaching five courses a semester.

Reflection questions for "Writing with a Heavy Teaching Load":

1. Why might faculty members at teaching-focused institutions be reluctant to write?

_____

_____

_____

_____

_____

_____

_____

_____

2. What are some other activities in your life, besides writing, that you need to schedule? How do you do it?

_____

_____

_____

_____

_____

_____

_____

_____

3. What kinds of sacrifices might faculty members be required to make in order to make time for writing?

_____

_____

_____

_____

_____

_____

_____

4. What are some of the benefits of being a working writer in addition to being a teacher?

_____

_____

_____

_____

_____

_____

_____

Part III

Essays on Thinking and Writing

27

The Case for Conversational Writing

Only once have I ever played the "I'm an English professor" card with any of my kids' teachers. That was when my middle son, then a high-school sophomore, received an F on a writing assignment that was clearly no worse than a B.

Up to that point, my son, a genuinely gifted writer, had made nothing but As in Language Arts. By the time he was in tenth grade, he had already guest-written my local newspaper column two or three times. He's now a junior in college, an English major (I know, I know) who aced two 300-level courses last spring.

The assignment in question gave students the option of writing an argumentative essay in the style of a newspaper editorial. For obvious reasons, that was the route he chose. I read through it before he turned it in and thought it wasn't his best work, but I decided getting a B might be good for him. It never occurred to me he would fail.

The teacher, when I met with her, acknowledged that the essay was well organized and virtually devoid of grammatical errors. So why had it gotten an F? Because, she said, the writing style wasn't academic enough.

I'm not going to tell you what was said after that, but you can probably imagine. Suffice it to say the story had a happy ending. But the incident got me to thinking, once again, about the difference between academic and conversational prose and the irrational bias so many writing teachers have in favor of the former. After all, I've heard some of my college-level colleagues voice similar complaints—that students don't know how to write academic prose.

My response to that is: Why should they? The fact that they're students, and that they're operating in an academic environment, does not make them academics. Nor will more than a fraction of them go on to become academics, thank goodness. The overwhelming majority won't be writing academic prose in their professional lives, so why should we be teaching it to them in college, much less high school?

This discussion is actually part of a larger debate about what constitutes good writing. I always tell my first-year composition students, when I'm trying to correct all the misconceptions about writing they've picked up in high school—you can't use personal pronouns or start a sentence with a conjunction, etc.—that the only reasonable standard for good writing is what good writers actually do. How many of our best nonfiction writers, the ones who are widely read and have a genuine impact, write in an academic style? Virtually none.

More to the point, how many professionals these days, apart from actual academics, write in an academic style? Again, almost none. Of course, lawyers and businesspeople have their own stylistic quirks, which can be even more annoying than academic prose. But the very best writers, in practically every field, avoid those quirks. They write in a conversational style.

Admittedly, there are conversations and there are conversations. Two academics talking to each other would sound very different from two corporate types, who would sound different from two restaurant managers or two custodians. Likewise, a college professor writing for students would sound different from a professor writing for other professors—or at least, that's how it should be, although many textbook writers seem to forget it.

What distinguishes a conversational style is not just that it's less formal (although it usually is) or that it avoids stuffy, made-up "rules" like the ones just mentioned (although it usually does), but that it attempts to approximate an actual conversation between a writer and a reader. In order to do that, the writer must first recognize that a reader exists, which academics often fail to do. Most scholarly writing (at least in the humanities) sounds to me like the writer is having a conversation with oneself. Perhaps that's consistent with the introspective, philosophical nature of the academic enterprise—let's not forget what the "Ph." in "Ph.D." stands for—but it doesn't translate well to the world outside of academia, which virtually all our students will inhabit.

Consider, for example, the following passage, which I chose more or less at random after surfing my college's online journal collection. (I'm not going to say where I got it, exactly, because my objective is not to criticize or embarrass anyone.)

> Last and highest on the thinking continuum is the evaluative type question that is considered a staple of published literature-based reading series. Usually found at the end of a story, this type of question requires student learners to offer their own opinions or evaluations….Some examples of evaluative questions for teaching literature include How are you similar to the character? What is your opinion of the character or events in the story? Why do you think the author wrote the story?...Bos and Vaughn (2002) similarly noted categories that help student learners distinguish between literal and interpretive questions—skills that they titled textually explicit, textually implicit, and scripturally implicit.

I say that I chose this passage "more or less at random" because I was looking specifically for something that would serve as a classic example of academic prose without being too egregious—which this isn't. It has all the earmarks of traditional scholarly writing: long, clunky sentences, passive voice, recurrent jargon. Yet the meaning itself is fairly easy to grasp, and I think most of us understand why it's written the way it is. As academic writing goes, this is better than some and no worse than most.

What this passage isn't, however, is engaging. I don't know about you, but the writer lost me midway through the first sentence. Speaking for a moment as a human being, not as an academic, I would read something like this only if I absolutely had to, and then I wouldn't be too happy about it. Ask yourself one simple question: After slogging through that short excerpt, do you have any desire to read the rest of the essay?

Me neither.

So why isn't the passage engaging? Because the author doesn't even try. He or she makes no attempt to engage a real live person who might be reading. It's almost as if that person, the reader, doesn't exist—as if the subject matter is so ponderously significant that it transcends any human interaction. That attitude, I've observed, is characteristic of academic prose, where the emphasis is typically on the ideas themselves rather than on communicating them effectively. You can either get it or not, the writer seems to be saying, and if you don't, that's your problem.

Now compare the previous passage to the following, from Malcolm Gladwell's bestselling book *Outliers*:

> The "achievement gap" is a phenomenon that has been observed over and over again, and it typically provokes one of two responses. The first response is that disadvantaged kids simply don't have the same ability to learn as children from more privileged backgrounds. They're not as smart. The second, slightly more optimistic conclusion is that, in some ways, our schools are failing poor children: we simply aren't doing a good enough job of teaching them the skills they need. But here's where Alexander's study gets interesting, because it turns out neither of those explanations rings true.

Now do you want to read more? Why? Because the writer has engaged you. And how did he do that? By varying sentence length to create a subtle sense of pace. By smoothing out the rough edges of the sentences through liberal use of contractions (generally considered a no-no in academic prose). By not only addressing readers directly but including us in the discussion ("our schools," "we … aren't"). By using simple, everyday words when such words carry the desired meaning, while not altogether avoiding longer words (like "phenomenon") when needed. "Simple," in this case, does not mean "simplistic."

Granted, Gladwell is one of the very best writers working today. But isn't that exactly what we ought to be teaching our students—what the best writers do? I've never bought the argument that professional writers have some sort of license the rest of us don't. That's like saying Steph Curry can execute a crossover dribble because he's Steph Curry, while the rest of us have to play like extras in a 1950 phys-ed film. I say if you can cross-over dribble, go for it. And if you can't, work on it until you can.

Even that analogy doesn't really illustrate my point, though, because what Gladwell does isn't fancier or more difficult. Granted, it's not easy to write as gracefully as he does, although he certainly makes it look that way. But the sort of conversational style he employs is, if anything, more natural and intuitive than what we spend years teaching students in high school and college. Perhaps the main reason students struggle to write conversationally is they've been told since kindergarten that it's not acceptable—even though it's perfectly appropriate for the vast majority of the writing they'll be doing throughout their lives.

I, for one, am here to tell them they can write conversationally, and they should. Because—speaking again as a human being, and as a reader—whether I'm perusing a scholarly tome or checking out the latest credit card offer in the mail, I'd much rather encounter a Gladwell wannabe than some pseudo-academic poser.

Reflection questions for "The Case for Conversational Writing":

1. What does it mean to say that writing is "conversational"?

_____

_____

_____

_____

_____

_____

_____

_____

2. What are some of the characteristics of academic writing? How do they affect the relationship between the writer and the reader?

_____

_____

_____

_____

_____

_____

_____

_____

3. Which style of writing should college writing classes be more focused on teaching? Why? Should they try to teach both? Why or why not?

_____

_____

_____

_____

_____

_____

_____

_____

4. Why do students struggle, sometimes, to write conversationally?

_____

_____

_____

_____

_____

_____

_____

_____

Accordions, Frogs, and the Five-Paragraph Theme

As a graduate student, I once drew a rather bad cartoon of an old schoolmarm (complete with Gary Larson–style beehive) standing in front of a class saying, "And when you finish your five-paragraph theme on 'What I Did Last Summer,' write a five-paragraph theme on. ... " The caption underneath read, "Janet Emig in Hell."

My attempt at humor had a small audience: fellow grad students in the rhetoric-and-composition program. To get the joke you have to be familiar with Emig's 1971 book, *The Composing Processes of Twelfth Graders*, which questioned prevailing methods of teaching composition. My classmates certainly got it: Emig's conclusions had been drilled into our brains, along with her disdain for one of the best-known artifacts of those traditional methodologies, the five-paragraph theme—an "essentially redundant form, devoid or duplicating of content," according to her.

That sort of indoctrination was typical of my "process oriented" education as a writing teacher. Formulaic constructs such as the five-paragraph theme, our professors told us, were mere crutches for writers too lazy to explore meaning on their own. Organization, they insisted, must arise organically from content. What's important, they suggested, is the writing process itself; the final product is all but immaterial.

At times, such propositions struck me as counterintuitive. The five-paragraph theme had worked well enough for me, after all, not just in freshman comp but, with some embellishment and expansion, even in graduate courses. I was also uncomfortably aware that my own success as a student stemmed largely from the fact that my written "products" were consistently judged to be outstanding.

But because everyone else—from the scholars whose works we studied to my professors and fellow students—seemed convinced that my attitudes were bourgeois and my experiences atypical, I concluded that I must be mistaken. The five-paragraph theme really was evil. And so, for years, I didn't teach it. Not in my freshman composition courses or anywhere else. In fact, I refused to teach it, even when students practically begged for a handy rubric to help them organize their thoughts. Instead, I attempted to lead them on a journey of self-discovery, or at least a discovery of what they were trying to say and how. To say that approach had mixed results would be to put the best possible spin on it.

Over time, real-life experiences began to challenge my comfortable, theoretical assumptions. First, I took a job in a state system that had a mandatory proficiency exam for rising sophomores, requiring them to (among other things) write a 500-word essay in an hour. So much for organization arising organically from content. In that kind of intensely stressful rhetorical situation, a crutch is exactly what most writers need.

Another eye-opening experience came when I took up technical editing on the side to pick up a little extra cash. What I discovered was that, first of all, people with graduate degrees don't necessarily write much better than college freshmen, but instead display many of the same problems. Moreover, I found that the most time-consuming part of turning something poorly written into something effective is reorganizing the material so the reader can follow the writer's train of thought.

Those experiences led me to conclude that, first, organization is a more important aspect of writing than I had realized; second, few people are naturally good at organizing their ideas in writing; and third, they're not going to magically become good at it over time, even if they're highly intelligent and well educated.

© Joanne Harris and Daniel Bubnich/Shutterstock.com

Welcome to My Classroom: ESSAYS ON THE FIRST YEAR OF COLLEGE

Such epiphanies, combined with the necessity of teaching the five-paragraph theme to students preparing for a writing-proficiency exam—and the success I had at it—led me to reconsider my antipathy toward the old standby. It is, after all, a relatively simple, easy-to-learn formula for organizing one's thoughts in writing. Moreover, it employs a widely used and highly effective approach to all sorts of communication, from after-dinner speeches to doctoral dissertations: introduction, body, and conclusion. As my freshman-comp teacher told us all those years ago, "Tell 'em what you're gonna tell 'em, then tell 'em, then tell 'em what you told 'em."

Of course, the five-paragraph theme is an artificial construct in the sense that, after our students leave freshman composition, most of them will probably never again write anything exactly like it. That's one obvious danger in relying on this format: Students will come to see it as the be-all and end-all of writing. But for the most part, we can lessen that risk by employing a couple of metaphors to which students can easily relate: the accordion and the frog.

The accordion metaphor explains how the five-paragraph theme must expand or contract to suit the writer's purpose and fit the rhetorical situation. For instance, a significant writing assignment for an upper-division course won't be five paragraphs in length; it might be twenty-five paragraphs or more. The introduction alone could take up three or four paragraphs, with another two or three devoted to the conclusion. That means the body of the essay will contain eighteen or more paragraphs, reflecting possibly five or six major supporting points, each of which needs three or four paragraphs to develop it.

On the surface, that seems a far cry from the five-paragraph theme taught in freshman comp, with exactly one paragraph of introduction, one of conclusion, and three in the body expounding three distinct points. But in reality, the format is the same, only expanded: more points, more development of each (the result, perhaps, of more research and in-depth thinking), and thus more paragraphs.

The same principle holds true for a fifty-page business proposal—an amount of information that might require two or three pages just to introduce and another page or two to wrap up. An interoffice memo, on the other hand, might be only three or four paragraphs long but will still require a brief introduction and conclusion, with the most important points sandwiched in between. The point is that, if students can learn to organize their ideas into five paragraphs, they should be able later on to expand or contract the format as necessary—especially if they understand that the five-paragraph theme is merely a beginning, not an end unto itself.

That's where my second metaphor comes in, that of the frog. A student who wants to become a heart surgeon doesn't start out by cutting people open. That student will probably begin, in an introductory biology course, by dissecting a frog. Over time, he or she may progress to cats or pigs, and beyond that, in medical school, to cadavers and eventually live patients. For student writers, the five-paragraph theme is their frog. It's not a ten-page term paper, much less a fifty-page proposal. But the lessons learned about organization from writing in the five-paragraph format make it possible, later on, to put together longer documents that are more logical and coherent.

Once we place the five-paragraph theme in its proper context, as an entry-level skill and not as an ultimate goal, we also find that it's pretty easy to answer Emig's concerns about redundancy. Yes, the format is naturally redundant. It's meant to be. But I don't really see that as a problem—and certainly not as a deal breaker—for a couple of reasons.

One is that redundancy itself isn't necessarily all bad. As any teacher, parent, or coach can attest, the way to get people to remember and improve at things is to repeat them over and over. Of course, that kind of constant repetition can become pretty boring. The trick is to repeat yourself without sounding as though you're repeating yourself—which can lead to many fruitful discussions about sentence variety, word choice, and the importance of vocabulary building.

Another concern often expressed by process-centered scholars and practitioners is that the five-paragraph theme is highly formulaic. Yes, it is—and so are most kinds of writing, from lab reports to sales letters to book proposals. One of the greatest favors we can do for our freshman writing students is to show them how to follow a set formula.

And what of Emig's contention that the five-paragraph theme is essentially devoid of content? Well, that may be true in many cases, but I don't think it's the format's fault. I'd guess that content issues probably have more to do with the writers' life experiences, or lack thereof. Personally, I find that the older students who often populate my classes seem to pack a lot of information into their five paragraphs. For the others, content should improve over time, as they continue their education, sharpen their interests, and gain more knowledge. Our job in the meantime is to help them acquire the tools they'll need to manage that knowledge, including a framework for communicating it to others.

It's true that what I'm advocating is a greater focus on the finished product, emphasizing traditional organizational patterns. But I don't see that as incompatible with teaching the writing process. Indeed, it actually reinforces the importance of the process, whose only real function, after all, is to produce a document that accomplishes what the writer set out to accomplish. More to the point, even if they're using a "crutch," writers still have to write and rewrite in order to iron out issues of grammar and syntax, logic and coherence, and idea development.

I don't mean to deny the possibility that some writers may, over time, move beyond formulas. They may develop the desire to explore meaning more deeply and discover for themselves how organization can derive organically from content. In fact, we have a name for such writers. We call them "professionals."

The vast majority of our students, however, will not become professional writers or anything close. If the best we can teach them to do is organize their ideas in a clear, logical manner, they will absolutely stand out from their peers—not to mention a few of the Ph.D.'s I've read.

Reflection questions for "Accordions, Frogs, and the Five-Paragraph Theme":

1. What exactly is the five-paragraph theme?

_____

_____

_____

_____

_____

_____

_____

_____

2. According to many experts, what are some of the problems with that type of writing? Why, specifically, are they problems?

_____

_____

_____

_____

_____

_____

_____

_____

3.   How does the "accordion" metaphor work to explain the value of the five-paragraph theme?

_____

_____

_____

_____

_____

_____

_____

4.   How does the "frog" metaphor work?

_____

_____

_____

_____

_____

_____

_____

Welcome to My Classroom: ESSAYS ON THE FIRST YEAR OF COLLEGE

29

Teaching as Unteaching

Is it just first-year composition instructors who have to spend half the semester correcting all the misconceptions students develop in high school? Or do faculty members in other disciplines encounter this problem, too?

For example, in the state where I live, the high-school language-arts curriculum requires that students begin each essay with a "thesis statement" that consists of four distinct elements: the thesis (or main idea) itself, plus three supporting points—all in the same sentence! The result, even when executed reasonably well, usually sounds something like this: "Smoking should be banned on all college campuses because it is unhealthy for individuals, creates an unhealthy and uncomfortable environment for all students, and produces large amounts of litter."

Where to begin cataloging the problems with that unfortunate construction? Let's start with the fact that not all topics lend themselves to such overt thesis statements, nor do all main ideas have exactly three supporting points. But even if you wanted your students to produce a traditional five-paragraph theme, with a clearly identifiable thesis and three distinguishable points, that is no way to go about it. Cramming all those elements together into a single sentence detracts from both thesis and support. It also produces an unnecessarily long and ungainly sentence with no clear focus.

In short, no editor in America would allow such a sentence to stand. It's simply bad writing. Why the high schools teach that approach is beyond me. But they do, and that means I have to spend an inordinate amount of time unteaching it. That requires a good deal of persuasion on my part, because by the time they get to me, many students are practically married to this stylistic atrocity.

And then there are the questions I'm constantly getting about what writers can and can't do in a piece of writing—even though I've attempted, over the years, to head off problems by answering these questions early in the term. Here are some of the most frequently asked questions, along with my (abridged) responses:

Students: Can we use "I"?

Me: If you're talking about yourself, of course you can. How else are you going to refer to yourself? In third person, like an NFL wide receiver? Just remember that we sometimes talk about ourselves more than we need to. If you find yourself doing that, the answer isn't simply to eliminate the pronoun—it's to edit out the extraneous or gratuitous self-references. But when you're illustrating a point by using an example from your personal experience, of course you can say "I."

Students: Can we use "you"?

Me: No, one cannot. Just kidding. The potential problem with "you" is that we sometimes use it to refer to people in general, and that isn't really what it means. But when you're addressing the reader—just as I'm addressing you right now—it's perfectly appropriate to say "you." The second person is also preferable when the alternative is some kind of hideous grammatical contortion adopted for no other purpose than to avoid that one pronoun. Something like, "One should always take one's books home with him or her so that he or she can study." (Shudder.) How about, "Be sure to take your books home so you can study." Much better.

Students: Can we use contractions?

Me: As a father of four, the best advice I can give you about contractions is this: When they're five minutes apart, it's time to get to the hospital. (Very few students ever get this joke, which I suppose is a good thing.) Seriously, you have to judge contractions on a case-by-case basis. Sometimes using a contraction makes you sound like you just wandered down out of the hills. Other times, not using the contraction makes you sound like one of those car dealers who was too cheap to pay a professional announcer to read his ad copy on the radio: "Come on down to Joe's Used Cars, where we are slashing prices. There is not a better deal in town." And understand that those two situations might occur in the same sentence. Generally speaking, contractions smooth out your sentences and make them more readable, but not always. Sometimes they cost you a little credibility.

Students: Can we start a sentence with a conjunction? End with a preposition?

Me: To quote Winston Churchill, "That is nonsense up with which I will not put." Seriously folks, the truth is that there's nothing you can't do in a piece of writing if you have a good enough reason. The corollary, the responsibility that accompanies the freedom, is that you should have a good reason for everything you do. If you happen to notice, in the editing process, that you began a sentence with "and," examine that sentence very critically. Ask yourself if it's really just a continuation of the preceding sentence and therefore ought to be attached. If not, maybe you can just drop the "and" altogether. Or maybe you need a slightly more forceful transition, like "moreover" or "in addition." Or maybe "and" works just fine for your purposes. There's nothing inherently wrong with using it to begin a sentence.

Students: But that's not what our high-school teachers told us. They said in college we'd have to …

Me: Well, this is college, and you don't have to. Hey, I remember my senior English teacher, back in 1978, making us do all sorts of things (like honest-to-goodness, bottom-of-the-page footnotes) because she insisted that's how we'd have to do it in college. Then I got to college and found out that wasn't the way we were supposed to do it at all. Maybe that's how they did it when she was in college in the 1950s. But I had to unlearn and relearn a lot of stuff. I guess you guys are in the same boat. You know what they say: The more things change, etc., etc., right? (Actually, most of them have never heard that saying, but that's OK.)

Those are just a few of the issues that I have to address every semester in my first-year composition classes. I'd certainly be interested to hear from students what other things they're being taught in high school (or elsewhere) that aren't really true—so I can get busy unteaching them.

Reflection questions for "Teaching as Unteaching":

1. What exactly is a "thesis statement"? What are "supporting points"?

_____

_____

_____

_____

_____

_____

_____

2. Why is it a bad idea to include a thesis statement and several supporting points all in the same sentence?

_____

_____

_____

_____

_____

_____

_____

3. What are some of the things that students are taught about writing in high school that do not turn out to be true once they get to college?

_____

_____

_____

_____

_____

_____

_____

_____

4. How can college writing instructors best address these misconceptions?

_____

_____

_____

_____

_____

_____

_____

_____

Welcome to My Classroom: ESSAYS ON THE FIRST YEAR OF COLLEGE

30

Editing Lessons

Talking about editing with my composition students the past couple of weeks has got me thinking about the way I edit my own writing, especially essays like this one that appear in *The Chronicle of Higher Education* and other local or national venues.

I know—you probably think I just dash these off without much thought, and some of my posts may have reinforced that impression. But I actually spend a great deal of time trying to get them just right. In *The Chronicle*, for example, I have a very large potential audience. There's no quicker or more thorough way to embarrass myself professionally, and perhaps personally, than by saying something really stupid in one of these posts.

Thankfully, I have wonderful editors whose job is to keep me from saying anything too stupid, and they usually succeed. Most of the time, they make me look like a much better writer than I really am, for which I'm grateful.

But even knowing that they have my back doesn't prevent me from editing obsessively. In fact, the longer I blog, the more obsessive I become, because I learn more with each post about the sorts of things I ought to be paying attention to. I no longer edit just for style and content, or merely to catch typos. I've learned that I have to do at least three other types of edits before I hit the "send" button.

First is the "fact-check edit," to make certain that if I've stated something as fact, it is indeed fact and I can prove it. I used to make statements, occasionally, that I just assumed everyone agreed with and accepted as fact, without offering any supporting evidence. These are blog posts, after all, not peer-reviewed journal articles—or so I reasoned. But I've figured out that you can't take anything for granted. A commenter (or twenty) is sure to ask, "Where's your evidence for that?"

Even in a blog post, if it's for an academic or professional audience, you'd better have a good answer. In fact, it's much better to provide the evidence up front, in the form of a link, before the opposition has a chance to pounce. Either that, or revise the statement so it's clearly offering an opinion or referencing general consensus, not stating a fact. And even then, unless the opinion is purely personal, it's not a bad idea to provide a link.

Next is the "liability edit," designed to make sure I don't get sued. I often employ experienced-based examples in my posts, as you may have noticed, but of course I've got to take great care that no one I depict in a negative light is identifiable—or at least that I've got plausible deniability. ("No, of course I wasn't talking about you.") I made the mistake a few years ago of skating pretty close to the edge a couple of times, and I was more than a little nervous for a few months afterward. Fortunately, the statute of limitations has long passed, but I don't want to deal with that kind of stress again.

Finally there's the "offensiveness edit," requiring me to read through the post one last time, asking myself if I've said anything that might offend anyone. This is the hardest edit of all, because it's becoming more difficult every day to predict what might be offensive. Sometimes the most innocuous-seeming throwaway lines end up angering some small group of readers that I had no idea existed and certainly didn't intend to set off.

The only surefire way to avoid all offense in a piece of writing is to place the cursor at the end and hold down the backspace key until all the text disappears. But of course I'm not going to do that. Instead, I've just got to try to be careful and, if I do inadvertently offend, apologize quickly in the comments section.

And if I advertently offend—well, at least I'll try to provide a link.

Reflection questions for "Editing Lessons":

1. Why is editing such an important part of the writing process?

_____

_____

_____

_____

_____

_____

_____

_____

2. Why is it so important to "fact check" what you write, especially for an academic or professional audience?

_____

_____

_____

_____

_____

_____

_____

_____

3. How can writers for the public sometimes get themselves in trouble, legally? How can they avoid that?

_____

_____

_____

_____

_____

_____

_____

4. Is it possible for a writer to avoid offending someone at some point? If so, how? And if not, what should the writer seek to do instead?

_____

_____

_____

_____

_____

_____

_____

Welcome to My Classroom: ESSAYS ON THE FIRST YEAR OF COLLEGE

31

"Three Things You Need to Work On"

As a college writing instructor for over thirty years, I'd like to share two key lessons I've learned as a parent that have greatly influenced both my teaching and, more importantly, my essay grading—the bane of every writing instructor's existence.

When my middle son was in elementary school, I used to coach his recreation-league basketball team every year. But at the end of one season, he took me aside and said, "Dad, I don't want you to coach my team anymore."

"Why not?" I asked, genuinely nonplussed.

"Because," he replied, "You're a lot harder on me than you are on the other kids."

"Oh," I said, in one of those moments of uncomfortable self-awareness that parents sometimes experience. By "Oh," what I really meant was, "Ouch."

So the next season, there I was in the stands with the other parents—and I was still coaching my son while he was on the court. That went on for about two games, until he came to me again and asked me to stop. "You're not my coach anymore, Dad," He said. "You can't keep yelling at me and telling me what to do during the game. It's too confusing. Plus, it's embarrassing."

Properly abashed, I agreed that, from then on, I would keep my mouth shut during the game except to cheer and offer general encouragement. Yet I still wanted to help. I knew my son loved basketball and longed to become a top player, and I believed my many years of playing and coaching experience could help him reach his goal. He recognized that, too, and wanted my help—just not in the way I'd been giving it.

So we talked about it and agreed that on the way home from each game, I could tell him three things that he needed to work on. From then on, he'd get in the car after the game and immediately ask, "OK, Dad, what are your three things?" He'd listen carefully, then work hard to make the improvements I suggested. He eventually went on to become an all-county high-school player.

Here are the two lessons I learned from that episode that I've since applied to my teaching and grading. First, when you're offering criticism to students—even remarks you regard as constructive—the way you say it is at least as important as what you say.

Covering a student's essay with red ink is the grading equivalent of yelling at that student. He or she will almost certainly feel belittled, inadequate, perhaps even humiliated. Worst of all, that student might not hear what you're saying. We all know how young people tend to shut down and tune us out when they feel all we're doing is berating them.

Second, I learned that students simply cannot process too much "advice," even if it's good advice, given with the best of intentions.

As a result, I don't mark students' essays with red ink. I use pencil instead. Moreover, I don't necessarily mark every mistake I see. Rather, I employ a version of the "three things" approach that served me so well with my son. I try to identify three (or four) key issues in a student's essay and, by my marks and comments, focus on helping the writer recognize and deal with those.

The issues themselves can vary greatly from student to student, and even for a particular student from one essay to the next. The point is, I'm trying to help all my students become better writers by overcoming specific weaknesses—a few at a time—rather than inundating them with every single thing they're doing wrong. Not many people can handle that kind of information overload.

I'm grateful to my son for teaching me that principle, all those years ago. It's made me a better writing instructor as well as a better parent. And my students, like my son, are profoundly grateful that I'm no longer yelling at them from the sidelines.

Reflection questions for "Three Things You Need to Work On":

1. In what ways is being a writing teacher like being a basketball coach? In what ways is it like being a parent?

2. In what way is covering a student's essay with red ink the equivalent of shouting?

3. Why is it important not to give too many pieces of advice all at once?

_____

_____

_____

_____

_____

_____

_____

4. Why is it important to treat each student as an individual and each essay as a separate piece of writing?

_____

_____

_____

_____

_____

_____

_____

32

Why I Dont Edit Their Rough Drafts

Like most professors who teach composition, I require my students to write multiple drafts—three, in fact—of each essay. That's not because three is a magic number. It's just a number that fits well with the amount of time we have in the semester, and it reinforces the idea of working through multiple drafts. If there is a "secret" to good writing, I'm convinced, multiple drafts is it.

And, like most of my colleagues, I regularly have students work in "peer editing" or "workshopping" sessions where they read and offer comments on one another's work.

None of this is groundbreaking pedagogy. In fact, it's pretty standard fare for a college-level writing course.

What I don't do, however—unlike most of my colleagues—is read all of my students' rough drafts before they turn in a final paper for a grade. Or maybe it would be more accurate to say that I don't edit any of their drafts, because I actually do end up reading a fair number. But I don't mark up each and every draft, and return it for revision.

That's enough of a departure from classroom norms that I can well imagine a lot of raised eyebrows at this point: "How can you not edit your students' drafts? What do you do with them, then?" My approach is a calculated strategy, designed to accomplish certain specific goals.

Workload management. Some readers may assume I'm just lazy—declining to read and edit students' drafts because it's simply too time-consuming. While I would dispute the first part of that statement—what you call "laziness," I would characterize as "workload management"—I do agree wholeheartedly with the second. Editing students' essays would, indeed, require many additional hours (that I don't have). More important, it's also unnecessary and even counterproductive.

But first let's run the numbers. Most semesters, I teach five composition courses, with 20 to 24 students apiece. They each write five essays, so I'm grading more than 500 essays every semester. Obviously that takes a lot of time. There's no way I could read, edit, and grade three times that many essays and still be able to fulfill my other professional responsibilities, not to mention have a life.

If I were going to edit students' rough drafts, I'd have to cut back on the number of papers they write (assign three instead of five) and probably cut back, too, on the number of drafts (two instead of three). Or I could use some version of the portfolio method, requiring students to continually revise the same two or three essays throughout the semester—as I know some of you do. That's a legitimate approach, and I have no problem with it.

Personally, however, I prefer to have students write more essays so we can cover a variety of genres. I also believe it's better for students to learn from their mistakes on an essay, put that one behind them, and move on to the next, rather than reworking the same piece until they (and I) are sick of it. (In lieu of a final exam, I allow students to revise one of their earlier essays and resubmit it for a higher grade.)

An audience they care about. One of the biggest obstacles to teaching writing skills is the inherent artificiality of the college environment. The classroom, after all, is not the real world. Nowhere else, outside of a classroom, do we find people writing essays for a grade.

An employee writing a report for a boss seems similar but there's a key difference: That boss might do any number of things with the report—praise it, ignore it, take credit for it, demand that it be rewritten. But one thing she won't do is mark it up with red ink and put a C- at the top. And that changes everything.

The pioneering composition scholar Donald Murray once observed that many composition mistakes simply disappear when writers care about their audience. When I first read that—some 30 years ago as a graduate student—I thought it couldn't possibly be true. Why would "caring" make errors go away? I have learned over the years, however, that Murray was exactly right: One of the keys to clear writing is a sincere desire for your audience to be able to understand what you're saying.

One of the best things I can do for my students, then, is to provide them with an audience that they just might care about. Clearly, that's not me; they don't care a whit about communicating with me, one human being to another. From me they only care about getting a good grade, which experience has taught them means minimizing errors—something that, paradoxically, makes them more error prone. (That's something all performers, from ballet dancers to closing pitchers, understand intuitively: You're much more likely to screw up if you're focused on not screwing up rather than on getting the job done.)

One of the main purposes of the workshopping is to provide students with a realistic audience of their peers—a group of people with whom they might actually wish to communicate. And one of the reasons I don't edit their drafts beforehand is so that students know their peer group will be the first to read what they've written.

Over time, students begin to write for each other—not for me—which leads to better writing.

Teacher versus editor. In recent years, I've done a fair amount of freelance editing—something quite different from teaching. The aim of an editor is to "fix" a piece of writing and make it suitable for publication—not necessarily to teach the writer how to do better next time (although that may be an important byproduct).

A teacher's main goal, on the other hand, is not to improve a particular essay but rather to help students grow and improve as writers. In that process, it is vital for them to learn from their mistakes and their successes—to find out for themselves, with our guidance, what works and what doesn't. Ideally, students will begin to make connections and recognize grammatical, structural, and thematic issues on their own.

That's less likely to happen if you as the instructor simply mark the errors, make some comments, and hand the paper back for the student to fix. In that scenario, students have no need to look critically at their essays; they know you are going to do it for them. Students are unlikely to make any changes beyond the ones you have suggested. In that scenario, they aren't learning much, they are simply exhibiting a Pavlovian response.

My rule is that I will read specific passages, upon request, and answer specific questions. But I won't read and edit an entire draft. That way, I make clear—by my actions, as well as my words—that they must learn to be their own editors and that they are ultimately responsible for the form and content of their essays.

The challenge here is that reading like an editor differs significantly from reading for information or enjoyment. Editing involves far more than just "fixing mistakes," or what you or I would call "proofreading." It requires seeing what's on the page while constantly thinking about what could have been on the page instead. It requires us to juggle, in our minds, multiple scenarios, in terms of diction, sentence structure, organization, and so forth.

That kind of thinking does not come naturally to most of us, and certainly not to most students. We have to train ourselves to do it. And what better way to help students develop that cognitive skill than to regularly put them in a position where they have to apply it, or at least attempt to? That, to me, is the main benefit of having students workshop their rough drafts in small groups: Students are, more or less, forced to think like editors.

Most of them aren't very good at it, at least at first, but they become more comfortable and adept. I start each workshop session with a 10-to-15-minute training module on some aspect of editing, helping them understand what to look for. By the end of the course they've become better at editing each other's work and, more important, their own.

All of those potential benefits are negated if we simply fix everything that's wrong with rough drafts. Students don't learn to improve their own writing, nor do they reap the rewards of helping others improve. Call me lazy, if you like, but that's why I don't edit students' drafts for them—and why I believe you shouldn't, either.

Reflection questions for "Why I Don't Edit Rough Drafts":

1. What is pretty standard about the author's approach to rough drafts? What's different?

    _____

    _____

    _____

    _____

    _____

    _____

    _____

    _____

2. What is the author's rule about reading student's rough drafts? Why?

    _____

    _____

    _____

    _____

    _____

    _____

    _____

    _____

3. Why is the concept of audience so important?

_____

_____

_____

_____

_____

_____

_____

4. What are some of the practical differences between a teacher and an editor?

_____

_____

_____

_____

_____

_____

_____

33

KISS (Keep It Simple, Stupid)

One of the most important things I learned as a young assistant basketball coach, from the grizzled veteran who became my first mentor, was the acronym "KISS." That stands for "Keep It Simple, Stupid"—and not, apparently, for "Knights in Satan's Service," as a local youth pastor asserted back in 1975, when I was still trying to figure out how the heck to play a vinyl LP backward so I could hear the hidden messages.

But I digress. The point my mentor was making is that even though basketball is basically a simple game, coaches have a way of making it more complicated than it has to be. That proved to be a valuable lesson throughout my coaching career, and it's been just as valuable to me as a writing instructor. Writing, too, is basically a pretty simple process—simple, not easy—but we have a way sometimes of overcomplicating it.

Nowhere is that more true, apparently, than in today's middle and high schools, where regular "writing assessments" are to harried teachers what annual colonoscopies might be to the rest of us. No doubt that's partly because all those teachers genuinely want to do a good job, but I imagine it's also because schools, and school systems, are essentially large bureaucracies, where everything is done by committee.

That means you have a lot of smart, dedicated people sitting around a table, all eager to contribute something to the lesson plan or the rubric or whatever. And all of them do contribute something, thus making the document about five times longer and more complex (let's be honest) than it really needs to be.

Recently I've had the opportunity to witness this firsthand, as my wife, who used to teach middle-school language arts back before our kids were born, is getting her toes wet again by filling in as a long-term substitute. One thing she shared with me is the acronym that they use—that they're required to use—to teach paragraph development to sixth graders: FRESQA (pronounced like the soft drink), which stands for facts; reasons and rhetorical questions; examples, explanation, and elaboration; statistics; quotes; and anecdotes and analogies.

That's a lot for a sixth grader to remember. Heck, it's a lot for me to remember. I had to ask my wife to run through it again for me as I was writing this post.

No doubt those are all good ways to develop ideas, but it seems to me that the acronym includes some overlap and maybe even redundancy (what's the practical difference between an example and an anecdote?), not to mention the fact that it lists ten items. Can you imagine some poor 11-year-old trying to tick those off on her fingers as time runs down during a high-stakes writing assessment?

Compare that to what I tell my first-year college composition students, which is that there are basically three ways to develop a paragraph: definition of terms, evidence, and examples. I think that sums things up pretty nicely, providing an adequate framework for talking about facts and assertions and statistics and anecdotes while involving only three things to remember instead of ten.

In fact, I can't imagine trying to teach my students something like FRESQA. I'm convinced that it would make the process much more difficult and confusing for them, rather than clearer and easier. Which brings us back to KISS. The more we think about something like writing (or basketball), the more complicated we tend to make it. But it doesn't have to be that way. Just keep it simple (I'm not going to call you stupid).

Reflection questions for "KISS (Keep It Simple, Stupid)":

1. Why do people—especially coaches and teachers—have a way of complicating things?

_____

_____

_____

_____

_____

_____

_____

2. What exactly does it mean to "keep it simple, stupid"?

_____

_____

_____

_____

_____

_____

_____

3. How might an acronym like "FRESQA" be helpful for students? How might it make things more difficult?

_____

_____

_____

_____

_____

_____

_____

4. Is there a simpler, more easily remembered way of expressing much the same idea?

_____

_____

_____

_____

_____

_____

_____

34

"To Be," or Not "To Be"?

So I had that conversation with my first-year composition class the other day—you know, the one about all the things you "should never do" in an essay, like use second-person pronouns (whoops) or begin a sentence with "but" or end one with a preposition.

I've come to expect some version of this conversation every semester. In fact, I spend a fair amount of time trying to disabuse students of such ill-conceived notions and get them to focus, instead, on what they can do in an essay. But I'm always amused at how the list of alleged cardinal sins in writing keeps growing.

One that has apparently been added in the last few years is "never use linking verbs," or forms of "to be." (Whoops, again.)

On one level, I understand why some of my students' previous teachers have told them that. I agree that overreliance on linking verbs tends to weaken writing. Most sentences benefit from stronger, more-specific verbs. But is it realistic to expect someone to get through an entire essay without ever using a linking verb? Obviously, I can't.

More to the point, has complete avoidance of linking verbs somehow become one of the new standards of "good" writing?

Not really. Not if some of our best contemporary writers are any indication.

Consider Malcolm Gladwell, a former staffer at *The New Yorker* and *The Washington Post* and author of several *New York Times* bestsellers. Gladwell is widely appreciated for his readability and conversational style, and he has a rare gift for making complex ideas accessible. If he's not one of our best writers, who is?

He's also, by the way, an essayist, which makes him especially relevant to this conversation, eliminating the "Well, you can get away with that in fiction" argument.

Here is an excerpt from *Outliers: The Story of Success,* one of Gladwell's best-known works (and, I might add, a fascinating read):

> For almost a generation, psychologists around the world have been engaged in a spirited debate over a question that most of us would consider to have been settled years ago. The question is this: is there such a thing as innate talent? The obvious answer is yes. Not every hockey player born in January ends up playing at the professional level. Only some do—the innately talented ones. Achievement is talent plus preparation. The problem with this view is that the closer psychologists look at the careers of the gifted, the smaller the role innate talent seems to play and the bigger the role preparation seems to play.

That seven-sentence paragraph contains, by my count, seven forms of "to be"—an average of one per sentence, although a couple of sentences have two and a couple have none. And, lest you think this is an isolated example—that I cherry-picked a passage in order to support my thesis—consider that on another page chosen entirely at random (page 150), I counted fourteen linking verbs in sixteen sentences.

Clearly, Malcolm Gladwell does not think it a crime to use linking verbs when he needs them in order to get his point across in a clear, concise, and readable way. And that leaves me wondering why we, or our students, consider it a crime.

After all, writing isn't mathematics, with hard and fast rules. The only reasonable standard for what constitutes "good writing" is what today's good writers actually do. If we're teaching our composition students anything other than that, then we're teaching something that is hopelessly antiquated, ridiculously elitist, severely limiting, or all of the above.

To be clear. Not long ago, I was myself taken to task by a reader for using too many linking verbs in an essay I wrote entitled, "What Makes a Good Leader?" I was arguing that faculty members don't necessarily mind being led; they just want to be led well. Here's the specific sentence with which the reader took issue: "Being led is one thing, but we don't want to be dictated to, we don't want to be treated like wayward children, and we don't want to be sold a used car."

"How many forms of the verb 'to be' does one sentence need?" the reader demanded to know. "Wasn't it William Zinsser who taught that verbs are the wheels of writing, and that they turn slowly when writers clutter sentences with 'be' verbs?"

OK, let's get something out of the way. I've read Zinsser's *On Writing Well* a couple of times. Liked it a lot. I've also read Strunk and White's *The Elements of Style.* And Orwell's "Politics and the English Language." And William Safire. And Stephen King's *On Writing.* Heck, like most writers, I've read everything about writing I could get my hands on, trying to find the secret. (Turns out there isn't one.)

So I pretty much know all the "rules." For the most part, I think they're reasonably good rules, even when they're not really rules. But my very, very favorite rule is Orwell's sixth: "Break any of these rules sooner than say anything outright barbarous."

So back to the offending sentence. True, it contains five forms of "to be." I agree: Generally speaking, that's a bad idea. It also employs the passive voice and ends an independent clause with a preposition—two other ostensible violations of "the rules."

But what are our options, in this case? Writers usually prefer the active voice because it clarifies meaning and eliminates unnecessary words—including, often, forms of "to be." In this case, I think the meaning of the sentence is perfectly clear, but can we eliminate some words? Let's try, using the active voice: "Faculty members don't mind someone leading them, but they don't want anyone dictating to them, they don't want anyone treating them like wayward children, and they don't want someone to sell them a used car."

Hmmm. That's actually thirty-five words, as opposed to thirty-two in the original sentence. Moreover, if we consider context, I wasn't simply talking about faculty members in the abstract; I was including myself among their ranks, using the first person. To retain that important (to me) element, we'd have to revise the sentence further: "As faculty members, we don't mind someone leading us, but we don't want anyone dictating to us, we don't want anyone treating us like wayward children, and we don't want someone to sell us a used car."

OK, that's better, in that it's more along the lines of what I was actually trying to say. Just one problem: Now we're up to thirty-seven words. The sentence also strikes me as, well, not barbarous, maybe, but at least a bit unwieldy. It's actually pretty close, by the way, to the sentence I started with, in my first draft. I played around with it and ended up changing it to its current form because I did think it was unwieldy, I suspected I could shorten it, and I decided the passive voice actually worked better in this case.

Yes, I agree with Zinsser (and Orwell, and others) that the passive voice and excessive use of "to be" are usually adulterants that weaken sentences. But not always. Each sentence has to be judged individually, on its own merits. For me, as a writer, the primary questions always are: "Have I said something worth saying? Have I said it as well as I can?"

So thanks to all of you who offer me writing tips. I do appreciate them, and I always try to pay attention and learn from them, even when they're given in a snarky, noncollegial, or sanctimonious manner. I just want you to know that I don't dash off these essays in half an hour. I spend a great deal of time working on each sentence, trying to get it just right. The fact that I rarely achieve "just right" makes me, I suspect, much like everyone else.

The unbearable obnoxiousness of "being." Whenever I have that conversation with students that I mentioned back in the first paragraph, about what you can and can't do in a piece of writing, I like to tell them there's literally nothing they can't do, provided they have a good enough reason (although if they're going to use the F-word, for example, or an ethnic slur, they had better have a darn good reason).

The corollary, I tell them—the responsibility that goes along with this freedom—is that they should think through and have a good reason for everything they do in a piece of writing. I believe that's sound advice, not just for first-year comp students but for writers in general.

However, having said all that, if I were Supreme Arbiter of the English Language and had the opportunity to eliminate one word—not merely ban it, but eradicate it entirely—that word would be "being." Not all forms of "to be," mind you. Just that one.

The main reason for my irrational and perhaps unhealthy antipathy toward this one word is that it's the primary culprit in what I've come to regard as the most egregiously obnoxious construction ever to defile an otherwise-acceptable sentence: "being that."

"Being that I was an only child …." "Being that the chapter wasn't supposed to be on the test …." "Being that my teammates looked up to me …." "Being that Poe was one of the greatest poets of the nineteenth century …." What all those sentences have in common is that the first two words make me not want to read the rest. In fact, they make me want to wad the essays up, douse them in lighter fluid, and set them ablaze while performing a ritual dance.

OK, that's going a bit too far. But as you may have deduced by now, I do not like that construction.

What's so bad about it? Let's start with the fact that it blatantly flouts Orwell's rule for conciseness, using two words where one will most certainly do. Clearly, when the writer says "being that," what he or she really means is "since" or "because." Think how much better the sentences above would read if the writer had simply said what he or she meant: "Since I was an only child …." "Because my teammates looked up to me …."

"Being that," by comparison, just sounds awful. It's an inversion, and a perversion, of a more common but only slightly better construction, "that being." I'm not a big fan of "that being," either, not least because in student essays it almost always signals a sentence fragment, with the verbal "being" substituted for an actual verb: "That being my favorite restaurant" instead of "That was my favorite restaurant." In addition, "that being," even if used correctly in an introductory phrase, often requires two additional words ("the case") in order to make any sense, thereby once again violating Orwell's dictate.

I'm sure there are times when "being" is a perfectly good and perhaps even indispensable word choice. I just can't think of any right now. And that being the case, I'm going to conclude this essay, being that I'm finished and all.

1. Name three things students are often told they can't do in a piece of writing. Are such prohibitions reasonable? What explanations are given for them?

_____

_____

_____

_____

_____

_____

_____

_____

2. Why is it often a good idea to avoid linking verbs, and how can writers accomplish that?

_____

_____

_____

_____

_____

_____

_____

_____

3. Is it possible to complete an entire, substantial piece of writing without using any linking verbs? Is it desirable? Why or why not?

_____

_____

_____

_____

_____

_____

_____

4. What's wrong with the construction "being that"? How can writers avoid it and do better?

_____

_____

_____

_____

_____

_____

_____

Dear Apostrophe: C Ya

Nearly thirty years ago one of my professors, talking about the way language evolves over time, predicted that the next evolutionary stage would involve common punctuation marks. Specifically, he said, the apostrophe would eventually cease to exist.

Think maybe I should send him a text to let him know just how accurate his prediction turned out to be?

As someone who teaches college writing to the text-messaging generation, I have observed that not only apostrophes but also capital letters have become, if not extinct, then at least increasingly conspicuous by their absence—sort of like some of my students when their essays are due.

I first began noticing this trend back in the mid-1990s, when email replaced the telephone as the most common form of interpersonal communication between two people not in the same room. And that was before everyone had a laptop, a tablet, or a smartphone (if not all three). These days, even people in the same room are more likely to communicate electronically than verbally.

The text-messaging revolution has exacerbated the situation. Personally, I've never quite understood the attraction of texting. Maybe that's because I'm still using my old Fred Flintstone signature-model flip phone, which I believe is made of water-buffalo horn and lacks a QWERTY keyboard. Thus I'm constantly having to push buttons multiple times. What a pain.

Couple that with the fact that the curmudgeonly English professor in me refuses to use abbreviations, substitute numbers for letters, or ignore the punctuation that I was so painstakingly (and painfully) taught in my youth.

And there, for me, lies the rub: do you know how many times I have to press the "1" key before I get to the apostrophe?

The upshot is that I seldom text, unless I'm in a situation where I have to communicate but can't call, such as when my kids are at school or I'm at the barber getting my ear hair trimmed.

For teenagers and young adults, though, it's different. They text while watching TV, while sitting in class, while driving, even while performing various bodily functions. (Yeah, I know. Too much information.) And so they're constantly using that handy texting shorthand, perpetually neglecting to capitalize, and consistently ignoring the apostrophe.

All of which would be fine if it applied only to text messaging. The problem, I fear, is that we're raising an entire generation of students who don't actually know that they're supposed to capitalize the first letter of the first word in a sentence. Who don't realize that the preposition "for" is spelled f-o-r. Who have never really learned—or at least rarely put into practice—the rule that a possessive or a contraction requires an apostrophe.

The result, as my professor foresaw long ago, is that we're losing a part of our language. Is it really that important, the apostrophe? I don't know. But I'm pretty sure my editor wouldn't have published this paragraph without four of them.

Reflection questions for "Dear Apostrophe: C Ya":

1. How does the English language evolve over time—and how is the apostrophe an example of that, potentially?

_____

_____

_____

_____

_____

_____

_____

2. In what ways have email and especially texting changed the way that many people—especially young people—use the language?

_____

_____

_____

_____

_____

_____

_____

3. What impact will that probably have, over time?

_____

_____

_____

_____

_____

_____

_____

_____

4. What other changes might we see to our language in the near future due to our increasing reliance on information technology?

_____

_____

_____

_____

_____

_____

_____

_____

Problem-Solving, Role-Playing, and the Rhetorical Situation

As a writing instructor, my greatest challenge is not underprepared students, online essay mills, or cell phones. It's the inherent artificiality of the classroom.

My first-year composition courses represent—for most of my students—the last concentrated writing instruction they will ever receive. So I try to equip them, as much as possible, for all the writing challenges they will ever face. I don't just mean for their college years, but also—and more important—for the next 40 or more years of their professional lives.

That's a tall order. In essence, I'm trying to prepare them for "real-world" writing in an environment—the college classroom—that is not "real world" at all. The problem becomes evident in class as soon as we start talking about audience. In my students' eyes, I am the primary audience for their essays, the only reader who really matters because I assign the grade. So naturally, they tend to write for me, which is completely unrealistic.

That rhetorical situation—a student writing an essay for a teacher—does not exist outside the classroom. An employee writing a report for a boss may be similar, in some respects, but there is at least one key difference: The boss might praise the report, criticize it, or not comment at all, but one thing he or she probably will not do is write all over it in red ink and put a C- at the top. That changes everything.

When students write for instructors, their primary goal is grammatical correctness. Communicating a set of ideas, one human being to another, becomes secondary (if that). And yet, the only legitimate purpose of writing, especially in a professional setting, is to communicate ideas.

Obviously, correctness contributes to clear communication, in the same way that following traffic rules helps a driver arrive safely at a destination. But the purpose of driving is not to obey the rules—it's to get somewhere. The same is true of writing.

The question, then, becomes: How do we create a realistic rhetorical situation for our students in this necessarily artificial environment?

One strategy I've found somewhat effective, as I've written before, entails dividing students into small groups to "workshop" or "peer edit" each other's rough drafts. My hope is that, over time, students in peer-editing groups will begin to write for each other and not for me. In this essay, I'd like to talk about another strategy I use—particularly with research-paper assignments—that I believe is even more effective in helping students learn to identify and write for a specific audience. It involves problem-solving and role-playing.

Let's be honest: Research-paper assignments in first-year comp courses tend to be on the lame side. Back when I was in college, my writing instructor assigned each student to write a research paper on a U.S. state. I got Montana. More recently, a former colleague of mine used to assign each student a year, like 1974 or 1982. Assignments like that raise an obvious question: What's the point?

Sure, by doing research on Montana—demographics, agriculture and manufacturing, the state bird (western meadowlark, in case you were wondering)—a student can learn to find sources, identify key pieces of information, integrate that information into an essay, and document everything correctly. Those are all important college-level skills, things students need to be able to do to succeed academically.

But does the assignment have to be so dry? Can't students learn the basic research and composition skills while writing about something that might have some relevance to them—that might, more to the point, resemble something a person would actually write about in their working life? (An aside: Some composition instructors try to get around the dullness factor by having their students write research papers about a work of literature. It's a more substantive approach but I don't use it because few of my students will become literary scholars.)

It's difficult to create a single assignment that encompasses all the different types of writing done in various professions. A research paper that takes a problem-solving approach gets around that dilemma nicely—since nearly everyone has to be proficient at problem-solving in their careers. I also ask students to identify both a realistic audience for their research paper and an appropriate role for themselves as writer, which usually requires a degree of role-playing. Let me explain how it works.

Problem-solving. The first thing I ask students to do when I introduce the research-paper assignment is think about a general field or subject area they would like to write about. It can be fairly broad at this point, and it can relate to their intended major or to some particular hobby or interest. The key is that it should be something personally important to them.

The next step is to identify a specific problem within the broad subject area. If that seems daunting, I remind students that they've already narrowed things considerably—going from all the possible problems in the world to problems in the field of, say, nursing. Or finance. Or athletics. I then suggest three ways for them to identify a specific problem to write about:

- Simply give it a bit more thought. The answer might be right there at the front of their brain.

- Do some light research. Read through publications or websites devoted to the topic to see what kinds of things people are talking about. That might give them potential sources, in addition to an idea.

- Talk to someone in the field. For example, I had a student several years ago who planned to become a physician and wanted to write her paper about something in the medical field, but she didn't know what. I asked her if she knew any doctors well enough to interview them. She had a brother-in-law who had just completed his residency and opened a practice in town. I said, "Perfect. Go talk to him." She ended up writing a paper about the challenges of opening a private practice and discovering there's a lot more to it than just treating patients.

The main thing I'm trying to get students to do, at this stage, is choose a topic that's genuinely meaningful to them—preferably one where they have some "skin in the game." I don't want them choosing a front-page-headline topic just because they think it will be easy to write about. As experienced writers know, that's usually an illusion. I'd rather not get yet another (frankly insipid) paper about climate change. I'd much prefer to read a thoughtful treatment of the parking problems on our campus, or the salary disparity between the NBA and the WNBA, or the out-of-control deer population in our state. And yes, I've had excellent papers on all of those topics.

Role-playing. Once students have defined a specific problem, the next step is for them to construct a realistic rhetorical situation, rather than the artificial student-writes-essay-for-teacher one. This is where we get into role-playing.

First, they must identify an audience. The operative questions are:

- Who would care about this problem enough to do something about it?

- Who actually could do something about it? That is, who could enact the solutions the student is planning to recommend?

In most cases, the answers to those questions will lead to a very specific audience. A student writing about combating bullying in elementary school, for example, needs to aim the essay at people who can actually do something about it, like teachers or administrators.

Hand in hand with audience goes the concept of the writer's role—essentially: Who are you as the writer of this paper? In real life, most people don't write long(ish), thoroughly researched, problem-solving essays. When they do write a report or white paper, it's because it's part of their job. So, for example, who would produce a document about how teachers should combat bullying in their classrooms? Maybe a counselor, a school administrator, or someone who works for a professional teachers' organization. Those are all realistic roles.

For the purposes of this assignment, the student must identify a realistic audience, adopt a realistic role, do enough research to play the role convincingly, and then write to that audience as if he or she were actually in that role.

Understand that none of that role-playing appears in the research paper itself. I'm trying to foster a frame of mind, a way of thinking. Just as I consciously think about my mom when I email her, I want students to consciously think about the audience they've identified. I do, however, require them to put all this information in a formal proposal—a separate assignment in which they define the specific problem they intend to tackle in their research paper, note some possible solutions, and spell out the rhetorical situation they've constructed, including the intended audience and their role as writer.

Many students find my research paper assignment odd, at first, and some have trouble grasping exactly what I'm trying to get them to do. But most eventually come to understand. The result has been papers that are much more focused and meaningful—to them and to me—than they would have been otherwise.

And even if students don't quite get the idea now, they will in five or six years, when they're writing this sort of thing for their supper.

Reflection questions for "Problem-Solving, Role-Playing, and the Rhetorical Situation":

1. What, according to the author, is the biggest problem he faces as a writing teacher? Why?

_____

_____

_____

_____

_____

_____

_____

_____

2. What are some research paper topics that, in the author's opinion, don't work? Why not?

_____

_____

_____

_____

_____

_____

_____

_____

3. What are some strategies students can use to identify a problem to write about?

_____

_____

_____

_____

_____

_____

_____

4. What makes someone, or some group, a realistic audience for a problem-solving paper?

_____

_____

_____

_____

_____

_____

_____

37

What Is Critical Thinking, Anyway?

The longer I teach (it's been well over 30 years, now) the more I'm convinced that the best thing we can do for our students is help them learn to think for themselves.

That involves explaining what critical thinking actually means—a step I fear we often skip—as well as equipping them with the requisite skills. That's why I recommend talking to students on the first day of class about critical thinking. What is it? Why is it important? How can they learn to do it?

What follows is an approximation of my opening-day remarks to students in my college writing courses. For graduate students and Ph.D.s new to teaching, if this explanation resonates with you, feel free to adapt it for your own classrooms.

These days, the term "critical thinking" has been overused to the point where it has almost ceased to mean anything in particular. It has become more of a popular educational catchphrase, so that even the people who use it often don't know exactly what they mean by it. Get any group of teachers in a room—kindergarten through college—and throw out the question, "What can we do to help our students learn better?" Within minutes, someone is bound to say, "I know, let's teach critical thinking!" Then another person in the group will say, "Oh, that's good. Write that down." And so they dutifully put it on the list, and everyone nods sagely, including the people who eventually read the list, and no one ever takes any concrete steps and nothing ever changes. This process is known as "educational administration."

None of that means, however, that critical thinking is not a real thing. It is—and it's vital for you to understand what critical thinking is and how to do it. The extent of your success in college—not to mention life—ultimately depends on it.

Critical thinking, as the term suggests, has two components. The first is thinking: actually thinking about stuff, applying your brain to the issues at hand, disciplining yourself (and it does require discipline) to grapple with difficult concepts for as long as necessary in order to comprehend and internalize them.

This is important because we live in a society that increasingly makes it easy for people to get through the day without having to think very much. We have microwaveable food, entertainment at our fingertips, and GPS to get us where we need to go. I'm not saying those things are bad. Ideally, such time-saving devices free up our brains for other, more important pursuits. But the practical effect is that we've become accustomed to setting our brains on autopilot.

Actual thinking requires deep and protracted exposure to the subject matter—through close reading, for example, or observation. It entails collecting, examining, and evaluating evidence, and then questioning assumptions, making connections, formulating hypotheses, and testing them. It culminates in clear, concise, detailed, and well-reasoned arguments that go beyond theory to practical application.

All of this, as I mentioned, involves discipline. And what better place to develop that discipline than in college courses, especially the ones you don't want to take because they're "not in your major"? After all, we can increase our brainpower, just as we can increase our physical strength, and in much the same way—by pushing against resistance. The greater the resistance, and the more we persist in pushing against it, the greater the intellectual benefit. That's why it's in your best interests to apply yourself to the courses you dislike the most and find most difficult: Those courses actually constitute "cross-training for the brain."

The second component of critical thinking is the critical part. In common parlance, "critical" has come to mean simply negative—as in, "I don't like to be around him, he's always so critical." But of course that's not what it means in an academic context.

Think of movie critics. They cannot simply trash every film they see. Instead, their job is to combine their knowledge of films and filmmaking with their extensive experience (having no doubt seen hundreds, even thousands of films) and provide readers with the most objective analysis possible of a given movie's merits. In the end, what we're left with is just one critic's opinion, true. But it's an opinion based on substantial evidence.

To be "critical," then, means to be objective, or as objective as humanly possible. No one is capable of being completely objective—we're all human, with myriad thoughts, emotions, and subconscious biases we're not even aware of. Recognizing that fact is a vital first step. Understanding that we're not objective, by nature, and striving mightily to be objective, anyway, is about as good as most of us can do.

To be critical also means to be analytical, to be able to look at a problem or question and break it down into its component parts—the way a chemist analyzes a compound. What makes a film good, or bad, or mediocre? Is it the acting? The directing? The script? The cinematography? All of them combined?

Finally—and perhaps most important—to be critical means to be dispassionate, to be able to separate your emotions from the situation at hand. That's not to say emotions are bad. Perhaps there are some decisions that, as human beings, we should make based primarily on emotions (although I would recommend giving your head a vote, at least). And we should certainly take emotional factors into account in all our decision-making, as in the case of compassion, for instance.

But in professional life, and to some extent in our lives in general, we simply can't make most decisions based primarily on emotion. We can't trust our emotions because they aren't necessarily grounded in reality. They are inconsistent, changing with our moods, with the seasons, with the time of day, with that last song we just heard on the radio—or the last presidential election. Emotions are, by definition, not based on reason and, therefore, form a poor, shaky foundation for decision-making.

Like thinking, learning to recognize and set aside our emotions requires a great deal of discipline. As humans, we're emotional creatures. Being dispassionate doesn't come naturally to us; we have to train ourselves to do it. And again, what better place than in a college classroom, where you're exposed to all kinds of ideas and information—including some you don't like?

Reflection questions for "What Is Critical Thinking, Anyway?":

1. Why should professors explain to students, early on, what "critical thinking" means?

_____

_____

_____

_____

_____

_____

_____

_____

2. Why do we need to be taught how to think?

_____

_____

_____

_____

_____

_____

_____

_____

3. What's the difference, if any, between teaching students how to think and teaching them what to think?

_____

_____

_____

_____

_____

_____

_____

4. What does the word "critical" mean in this context?

_____

_____

_____

_____

_____

_____

_____

Welcome to My Classroom: ESSAYS ON THE FIRST YEAR OF COLLEGE

Why College Graduates Still Can't Think

Several years have passed since Richard Arum and Josipa Roksa rocked the academic world with their landmark book, *Academically Adrift: Limited Learning on College Campuses*. Their study of more than 2,300 undergraduates at colleges and universities across the country found that many of those students improved little, if at all, in key areas—especially critical thinking.

Since then, some scholars have disputed the book's findings—notably, Roger Benjamin, president of the Council for Aid to Education, in a 2013 article entitled, "Three Principle Questions about Critical Thinking Tests." But the fact remains that the end users, the organizations that eventually hire college graduates, continue to be unimpressed with their thinking ability.

In 2010, the Noel-Levitz Employer Satisfaction Survey of over 900 employers identified "critical thinking [as] the academic skill with the second largest negative gap between performance satisfaction and expectation." Four years later, a follow-up study conducted by the Association of American Colleges and Universities found little progress, concluding that "employers…give students very low grades on nearly all of the 17 learning outcomes explored in the study"— including critical thinking—and that students "judge themselves to be far better prepared for post-college success than do employers."

As recently as May of 2016, professional services firms PayScale and Future Workplace reported that 60 percent of employers believe new college graduates lack critical thinking skills, based on their survey of over 76,000 managers and executives.

Clearly, colleges and universities across the country aren't adequately teaching thinking skills, despite loudly insisting, to anyone who will listen, that they are.

How do we explain that disconnect? Is it simply that colleges are lazily falling down on the job? Or is it, rather, that they're teaching something they call "critical thinking" but which really isn't?

I would argue the latter.

Traditionally, the "critical" part of the term "critical thinking" has referred not to the act of criticizing, or finding fault, but rather to the ability to be objective. "Critical," in this context, means "open-minded," seeking out, evaluating and weighing all the available evidence. It means being "analytical," breaking an issue down into its component parts and examining each in relation to the whole.

Above all, it means "dispassionate," recognizing when and how emotions influence judgment and having the mental discipline to distinguish between subjective feelings and objective reason—then prioritizing the latter over the former.

I wrote about all this in a recent post on *The Chronicle of Higher Education's* Vitae website, mostly as background for a larger point I was trying to make. I assumed that virtually all the readers would agree with this definition of critical thinking—the definition I was taught as a student in the 1980s and which I continue to use with my own students.

To my surprise, that turned out not to be the case. Several readers took me to task for being "cold" and "emotionless," suggesting that my understanding of critical thinking, which I had always taken to be almost universal, was mistaken.

I found that puzzling, until one helpful reader clued me in: "I share your view of what critical thinking should mean," he wrote. "But a quite different operative definition has a strong hold in academia. In this view, the key characteristic of critical thinking is opposition to the existing 'system,' encompassing political, economic, and social orders, deemed to privilege some and penalize others. In essence, critical thinking is equated with political, economic, and social critique."

Suddenly, it occurred to me that the disconnect between the way most people (including employers) define critical thinking and the way many of today's academics define it can be traced back to the post-structuralist critical theories that invaded our English departments about the time I was leaving grad school, in the late 1980s. I'm referring to deconstruction and its poorer cousin, reader response criticism.

Both theories hold that texts have no inherent meaning; rather, meaning, to the extent it exists at all, is entirely subjective, based on the experiences and mindset of the reader. Thomas Harrison of UCLA, in his essay "Deconstruction and Reader Response," refers to this as "the rather simple idea that the significance of the text is governed by reading."

That idea has been profoundly influential, not only on English faculty but also on their colleagues in the other humanities and even the social sciences. (Consider, for example, the current popularity of ethnography, a form of social science "research" that combines fieldwork with subjective story-telling.)

Unfortunately, those disciplines are also where most critical thinking instruction supposedly occurs in our universities. (Actually, other fields, such as the hard sciences and engineering, probably do a better job of teaching true thinking skills—compiling and evaluating evidence, formulating hypotheses based on that evidence, testing those hypotheses for accuracy before arriving at firm conclusions. They just don't brag about it as much.)

Welcome to My Classroom: ESSAYS ON THE FIRST YEAR OF COLLEGE

The result is that, although faculty in the humanities and social sciences claim to be teaching critical thinking, often they're not. Instead, they're teaching students to "deconstruct" to privilege their own subjective emotions or experiences over empirical evidence in the false belief that objective truth is relative, or at least unknowable.

That view runs contrary to the purposes of a "liberal arts" education, which undertakes the search for truth as the academy's highest aim. Indeed, the urge to deconstruct everything is fundamentally illiberal. Heritage Foundation's Bruce Edwards calls it "liberal education's suicide note" in that it suggests the only valid response to any idea or situation is the individual's own—how he or she "feels" about it.

Unfortunately, such internalization of meaning does not culminate in open-mindedness and willingness to examine the facts and logic of differing views. Rather, it leads to the narrow-minded, self-centered assumption that there is a "right" way to feel, which automatically delegitimizes the responses of any and all who may feel differently.

All of this has a profound impact on students and explains a great deal of what is happening on college campuses today, from the dis-invitation (and sometimes violent disruption) of certain speakers to the creation of "safe spaces" complete with Play-Doh and "adult coloring books" (whatever those are—I shudder to think). Today's students are increasingly incapable of processing conflicting viewpoints intellectually; they can only respond to them emotionally.

More to the point, that explains why employers keep complaining that college graduates can't think. They're not being taught to think. They're being taught, in too many of their courses, to "oppose existing systems"—without regard for any objective appraisal of those systems' efficacy—and to demonstrate their opposition by emoting.

That may go over just fine on the quad, but it does not translate well to the workplace.

Reflection questions for "Why College Graduates Still Can't Think":

1. What are some of the complaints employers have with new college graduates?

_____

_____

_____

_____

_____

_____

_____

_____

2. In what way does that constitute a "disconnect" with what colleges claim to be teaching?

_____

_____

_____

_____

_____

_____

_____

_____

3. What has the phrase "critical thinking" traditionally meant?

_____

_____

_____

_____

_____

_____

_____

4. What supposedly is the purpose of a liberal arts education? Why is critical thinking important in that context?

_____

_____

_____

_____

_____

_____

_____

39

Competing Facts Are a Fact of Life

"Alternative facts" have gotten quite a bad rap lately, which—while understandable—is a shame. Because virtually any argument worthy of the name involves competing sets of facts. That's why it's an argument, not a hug-fest. And to pretend otherwise is actually counterproductive, especially if we want our students to be able to engage in constructive arguments.

Take trial lawyers, for example. To exonerate their clients, defense attorneys often present alternative theories, based on alternative facts, most of which are actually facts. Perhaps the accused can prove he was never at the crime scene, even though his blood was found on the victim. In its deliberations, the jury must weigh these seemingly disparate facts—although what they may really be judging is which lawyer made the better argument. Much the same is true of political debates.

My purpose here is not to weigh in on any particular point of view but merely to point out: (1) In a debate, one camp rarely has all the facts on its side, or even in its possession; and (2) although we often use the words "fact" and "truth" synonymously, they are not the same thing.

As faculty members, we must be careful lest our students get the false impression that they can go into an argument as the only ones who have "the facts." Such intellectual arrogance leaves them ill-prepared for the rigors of actual debate and sets them up for failure. Instead, no matter how heated the rhetoric becomes, we must persist in the grand liberal-arts tradition of teaching students how to evaluate the validity of various points of view, how to gather data through research, how to analyze that data, and how to counter fact-based arguments (or ostensibly fact-based arguments) with facts and rhetorical strategies of their own.

Our students need to understand that there are myriad ways in which information can be both factual and dead wrong (remember, for example, the parable of the blind men and the elephant). In most serious debates, both sides have actual facts to bolster their arguments. But how those facts are interpreted, how accurate they are, whether they're relevant to the issue at hand, whether they're actually significant, and whether they represent the whole truth—those are all separate questions.

Answering such questions is what scientists, social scientists, and (yes, even) humanists do every day. It's the reason people do research, and the reason peer-reviewed journals exist—so scholars can learn from each other, add to their knowledge, expose faulty hypotheses (their own and others), all while moving toward a better and deeper understanding of the issues under discussion. This is known as progress.

For both us and our students, two things can happen if we honestly examine the other side's arguments rather than simply dismissing them as false because they don't comport with our beliefs. One is that we might end up modifying our views, recognizing that—even if we still disagree—some of what our opponent is saying is actually valid.

The other benefit of understanding our opponents' arguments is that we can then decide how best to counter them.

For example, when I was a department chair, I had to fight every year for my unit's share of scarce resources, including money for new full-time faculty positions. That often meant arguing that my department needed an additional English professor more than the science department needed another biologist. I made my arguments based on data—how many sections we offered, how many were staffed by part-timers, and how many were cancelled because we couldn't find an instructor. Meanwhile, the science chair was making her case in exactly the same way. Neither of us was lying or distorting the data. We both had legitimate needs, along with verifiable facts to support our positions. But if there was only one faculty line for the two of us, the dean had to weigh our competing sets of facts, and make a decision in the best interests of the institution.

More to the point, rhetorically speaking, my success as chair depended in large part on my ability to procure resources for my department. That meant making persuasive, fact-based arguments while recognizing that those with different agendas were also making arguments using other sets of facts.

So, yes, there really is such a thing as alternative facts. Sometimes, as has been noted, they're not really facts but rather lies, distortions, deceptions, or obfuscations. But many times they actually are facts, and refusing to acknowledge that does us no good if we want to win the argument, much less arrive at the truth, whether in the classroom or in life.

Reflection questions for "Competing Facts Are a Fact of Life":

1. What are "alternative facts," and why have they gotten a bad rap lately?

_____

_____

_____

_____

_____

_____

_____

2. Can you think of a situation, besides the ones mentioned, where competing facts might come into play?

_____

_____

_____

_____

_____

_____

_____

3. In what way are "facts" and "truth" not necessarily the same thing?

_____

_____

_____

_____

_____

_____

_____

4. Why is it important for students to understand that one side in an argument rarely has all the facts?

_____

_____

_____

_____

_____

_____

_____

Welcome to My Classroom: ESSAYS ON THE FIRST YEAR OF COLLEGE

© Kolett/Shutterstock.com

Part IV

Essays on Issues in Higher Education

40

The Good That Community Colleges Do

In a classic case of dueling studies, the American Association of Community Colleges recently issued a report showing that most community-college students see a significant return on their financial investment. That was in response to an earlier report, produced by the American Institutes for Research, indicating that for some students, the value of a two-year degree is less than that of a high-school diploma.

The release of those two apparently contradictory studies within a few months of each other prompted a fair amount of finger-pointing, thinly veiled accusations, and claims and counterclaims. In other words, it was business as usual in the dog-eat-dog world of higher-education policy debate.

I don't doubt that both groups had the best of intentions, and that both reports make valid and important points that policy makers would do well to consider. I applaud both efforts to evaluate what community colleges do in concrete terms because I understand that in our current regulatory environment, such empirical measures are necessary.

And yet, as someone who has worked at community colleges and other access institutions for thirty-plus years, I can't help but think that neither study manages to tell the real story. Because the truth is, so many of the things that community colleges do for their students and communities are difficult to measure empirically. Here are a few of the things I have in mind.

Open doors. Most two-year colleges around the country maintain open-door policies, meaning that they accept any students with a high-school diploma or GED, regardless of their grades or test scores. Some even offer GED programs onsite, so that students who want to attend college but never finished high school can do so.

It's true that many of those students—OK, most of them—place initially into precollege, "developmental studies" courses, designed to improve their academic deficiencies and bring them up to college-level work.

I don't necessarily disagree with those who say, "They should have learned those things in high school." Of course they should have. But the fact is, many students didn't. Maybe they were just lazy and unmotivated at the time, as teenagers can be. But maybe their high schools were subpar. Or maybe they had personal or family issues that interfered with their studies. In any case, there's nothing community colleges can do except help those students try to overcome their deficiencies. If they're willing to put in the time and effort, so are we.

I should note that some debate the benefits of developmental studies. Many believe, and some research indicates, that certain students actually do better when they go straight into college-level courses, despite placing into developmental courses. Other students, however, clearly do not have the skills for college work, especially in math and reading.

It's also true that, for students who start out in developmental studies, graduation and transfer rates are very low—less than 30 percent, according to some studies.

But for me, the real question is not "How many students who began in developmental studies went on to earn a college degree?" It's "How many of those students would have ever earned a college degree if it weren't for a local community college that offered them courses and support?" I suspect the answer is somewhere not far north of zero.

We often hear politicians and pundits talk about "equality of opportunity," as opposed to equality of outcome. Fair enough. They ought to be big fans of community colleges, then, because that's exactly what our colleges provide: opportunities for those who wouldn't otherwise have them. What students do with those opportunities is up to them.

Second chances. There's another group I didn't mention on my shortlist of academically deficient students: the ones who haven't seen the inside of a high school in a decade or more. They are either entering college for the first time or going back after dropping out years earlier. Maybe they've been in low-wage jobs and want to increase their earning power. Maybe they've been raising a family and haven't had time for school. Or maybe they just want to fulfill a lifelong dream of earning a college degree and entering a specific profession, like nursing.

For many of them, starting out at a four-year university is out of the question. Besides whatever academic weaknesses they might have after years away from the classroom, they're also intimidated by the admissions process and by the idea of having to take, or retake, a college entrance exam. For them, community colleges, with their open-door policies, are a perfect fit.

That's why the average age of community-college students, despite falling slightly in recent years, has hovered in the upper twenties for nearly three decades. What other type of public institution can say that?

I would be remiss if I did not mention one last group of students that benefits from the second chances our colleges offer: those who go off to a university right after high school and find themselves in over their heads—socially, academically, or both.

My college, like most two-year campuses, sees a fair number of such students each fall. A year earlier, they would not have given us a first glance, much less a second. Now they're "back home," trying to get their grades up so they can return to the university. And a fair number of them do make it back. But how would they do so without us?

Early entry. At the other end of the spectrum from the students who aren't ready for college when they graduate from high school are the ones who find themselves ready long before they graduate. Community colleges offer those students early-college programs that go by many different names but are mostly referred to as "dual enrollment."

Community colleges aren't the only institutions that offer dual-enrollment courses, but in many states they are the primary providers of such programs. My own two-year college has, by far, the largest dual-enrollment population in the state, with more such students than the top four state universities combined.

I've been teaching these courses since I first began in this business. I've also helped to administer our dual-enrollment program, and I have three kids who have gone through it. As far as I'm concerned, it's one of the best-kept secrets in American higher education, and I don't understand why more families don't take advantage of it.

Although some critics have questioned whether dually enrolled students are getting ahead of themselves, my experience has been that the vast majority are indeed ready for college. Most end up transferring their credits to state universities, where they do quite well. Arriving with up to a year of college-level work under their belts, they are much better prepared for the academic rigors of university life than typical freshmen are. Meanwhile, because the state picks up most of the tab, the financial savings to them and their families can be considerable—and, in many cases, quite welcome.

Once again, without the local two-year college, far fewer people would have the opportunity to reap those benefits.

Economic value. Dually enrolled students aren't the only ones who save money by starting their higher education at a community college. In many states, tuition and fees at two-year institutions are less than half what students would pay at a four-year university, and they can save even more by living at home.

Considering the vast and growing amount of student debt, that's not a bad option. In fact, if it weren't for community colleges, tens of thousands of our high-school graduates probably wouldn't be able to afford college at all.

I know what some of you are thinking: You get what you pay for. It's probably true that, as some studies have shown, the quality of a community-college education can vary from state to state and from campus to campus. But generally speaking, most community colleges these days are either part of the same state system as four-year institutions, or else have detailed articulation agreements with them. Either way, representatives from both two-year and four-year campuses have probably spent years working through quality-control issues by developing common course numbering systems, outlines, and standards.

In other words, in most states, English 101 at the local community college is the same course as English 101 at the state university.

Moreover, community colleges actually offer students certain advantages, academically speaking. For one thing, class sizes tend to be much smaller in most core courses. Instead of 400 people in your biology lecture at a university, for instance, you are more likely to have 40 in that same class at a community college. And whereas many entry-level courses at the university are taught by relatively inexperienced graduate students, most of those same classes at the community college are taught by well-qualified, seasoned instructors.

© bikeriderlondon/Shutterstock.com

I'm not saying community colleges are better overall when it comes to general education than four-year universities. I'm not even necessarily saying we're better for most students. But it's clear that we're the better choice for many students, and the only way they will have the opportunity to earn a degree.

As a visiting dignitary once said of my two-year college during commencement, "If this institution did not exist to serve this community, somebody would have to invent it."

Points of access. In April 2014, *The Chronicle* reported on a new study on "The Effects of Rurality on College Access and Choice," which found that students in rural areas are less likely to go to college. Those who do go to college, the study said, "are more likely to choose two-year institutions"—as if that were a bad thing.

Perhaps rather than wringing our hands over the fact that some students can't attend four-year institutions, we ought to be grateful that community colleges exist for those students. Because if people have access to a community college, then they have access to college. Community colleges are colleges. And the authors of the study are correct in suggesting that they are sometimes the only colleges to which residents have ready access.

That's not just true in rural areas, by the way. Community colleges can also be found in many urban neighborhoods where students can't easily get to a four-year campus. With the local two-year college right down the street, they can walk to class rather than having to take a bus or live away from home. That's a huge advantage for untold thousands of students, and the only reason that many of them are able to go to college at all.

The two-year college where I teach sits in a sprawling suburb, where the nearest state university is at least twenty miles away. Students who don't want (or can't afford) to make that drive in Atlanta traffic come to us. Students at nearby high schools who wish to take dual-enrollment courses come to us. College kids home for the summer, or home temporarily after "flunking out," come to us. If we weren't here, taking college courses would suddenly become a much greater hardship, even for some relatively affluent students.

For decades, community colleges across the country have made going into underserved areas something of a specialty, opening branch campuses in remote locations, teaching night classes at local high schools and community centers, offering distance learning in various formats. In many cases, they form partnerships with four-year institutions so that students can go on to earn bachelor's degrees. Some community colleges have even gotten into the bachelor's-degree business themselves.

The point is: One of the best things that community colleges do for their communities, often with little or no recognition, is to provide access to higher education for populations that wouldn't otherwise have it.

Community repositories. I gave a lot of thought to the heading for this section, looking for a phrase that would encapsulate all the many ways in which two-year colleges serve as focal points for their surrounding towns and cities.

I thought of "community center," but of course that term has other connotations. In many communities, the local two-year college is indeed a center—for the arts and performing arts, for science and business, for athletics and fitness. There are plenty of places across the country where people would rarely get to see a play or an orchestra, attend a college-level sporting event, find an inexpensive gym, or attend a seminar on starting a small business if it weren't for the local community college.

But community colleges aren't just places for local residents to go; faculty and staff members also become emissaries to the local community. In many parts of the country, the best-educated people around, the most knowledgeable on a wide range of topics, work at the community college. When a civic club or church group needs a speaker, or the high school needs judges for a science fair, or the senior center needs someone to teach pottery, or the garden club needs a botanist, they all go to the local community college.

Call it community outreach if you like, but this is another key element of their mission that community colleges, and the people who work there, enthusiastically embrace.

Learning laboratories for higher education. Community colleges are not graduate schools of education—the sort of places where important research discoveries are made or theories about learning are developed. But two-year colleges are often the places where discoveries and theories about teaching are most enthusiastically greeted, as well as the places where they are initially, and perhaps primarily, put into practice.

Teaching is our mission. As faculty members, we are constantly looking for new and better classroom strategies. The vast majority of professional-development opportunities on our campuses have to do with how to improve teaching. More than any other type of institution, community colleges have embraced the teaching-and-learning movement and perfected online learning (insofar as it can be perfected).

By testing classroom innovations, using hundreds of thousands of live subjects every year, community colleges provide a wealth of data for the rest of the education community—including those graduate schools of education—regarding what actually works and what doesn't work.

Workforce developers. On more than one occasion, I've objected to the perception that two-year colleges exist primarily to provide "workforce development," by which people usually mean technical degrees. That characterization, I've long believed, overlooks the vital role that community colleges play in teaching core academic courses to students who plan to transfer to four-year institutions. A recent study found that, among American university graduates in 2010 and 2011, just under half attended a two-year college at some point. That means community colleges now provide the liberal-arts foundation for a growing number of our future teachers, doctors, lawyers, and business leaders.

That said, community colleges do perform an indispensable service for their regions by offering courses, degrees, and certificates in high-demand technical fields like information technology, health science, and construction management. In addition, they often play a vital and unique role in offering highly specialized training targeted at specific industries. If a manufacturer builds a new plant in town, business leaders can always count on the nearest community college to step up and provide the courses necessary to train or retrain workers.

That obviously benefits those workers, but it also benefits communities by helping them attract industry and then provide those companies with skilled workers.

Economic engines. Given the role that they play in workforce development, and the simple fact that they now enroll roughly a third of all college students nationwide—which means they have to employ a lot of people to teach and support those students—community colleges are obviously vital to their local economies. And when I say "vital," in this case, that's not hyperbole.

Take my institution, Perimeter College. It's moderately large for a two-year college—around 23,000 students—and located in a thriving metropolitan area that also includes more than a dozen four-year institutions. According to state data, my college had an economic impact in 2012 (the most recent year for which statistics are available) of $774 million, providing more than 7,200 jobs. I've worked at a handful of community colleges, and two of them, one in a small city and the other in a rural area, were the largest employers in their region. That is not uncommon.

Without the local community college, what would those regions do? How would they replace all those jobs? Where would their kids—and for that matter, their adults—go to college? Where would residents go to find subject-matter experts, or to watch a play, or to attend a seminar? What would attract industry to an area that could not promise a trained workforce?

No doubt that's what that speaker meant when he said that if community colleges didn't exist, somebody would have to invent them. Fortunately they do exist. Because without them, many communities would be far, far poorer places.

Discussion questions for "The Good That Community Colleges Do":

1. What are some of the reasons that two-year colleges and other access institutions don't get as much attention or respect as four-year schools?

_____

_____

_____

_____

_____

_____

_____

_____

2. What are some of the ways that two-year colleges can benefit individual students?

_____

_____

_____

_____

_____

_____

_____

_____

3. What are some ways that they can benefit communities?

_____

_____

_____

_____

_____

_____

_____

4. How does the existence of two-year and access institutions benefit American higher education?

_____

_____

_____

_____

_____

_____

_____

41

The Completion Conundrum

Last August my colleagues and I were told in a faculty meeting that if we didn't make sure our students graduated then we weren't serving them well.

With all due respect, that's nonsense.

To be fair, that comment came from someone who has an unenviable task: leading our two-year college's response to the state's "Complete College Georgia" plan, which is aligned with the national College Completion Agenda. Further complicating matters is the fact that our state funding—never exactly a windfall to begin with—will now depend, in part, on how well our students "complete," which apparently means "graduate with a credential."

I understand what's driving this agenda. No one denies that today's sophisticated economy requires a better-educated populace. At the same time, recent studies indicate that the United States lags behind other industrialized nations in graduation rates. Two-year colleges, in particular, seem to have a poor track record when it comes to graduating their students. It's easy to see how policy makers, especially during an anemic recovery, might wonder if continuing to finance such "failure" is a wise use of resources.

Those of us who view teaching as a calling would obviously love to see more of our students succeed in reaching their educational goals. And when they don't, we, to some degree, do feel responsible. But it's not as though we haven't been trying. What we used to call "retention" has been an issue for as long as I've been around academe. During my twenty-nine-year career, I've gone through more retention "initiatives" than college presidents, and that's saying something.

In other words, this is not a new problem. What's new is the proposed solution in my state and many others: to reduce a college's funding if it doesn't measure up to arbitrary standards of completion.

Will that motivate faculty members to try harder? Maybe. Or maybe they've already been trying as hard as they can, and they'll just throw up their hands and wait for the inevitable (which, to some extent, is what I'm seeing). Or maybe they'll simply "improve" completion by lowering standards, which will give us more graduates who know less. That's a fairly common response when teachers are faced with unrealistic expectations coupled with punitive measures.

My plea, aimed primarily at legislators and policy makers at the state level, is to exercise good judgment when crafting and enforcing college-completion policies. Please take time to educate yourselves about the different types of academic institutions in your state and their respective missions, lest you do irreparable harm through well-meaning attempts to regulate something that may, in the long run, prove impossible to regulate.

To that end, I would like to offer five truths about two-year colleges that I hope policy makers will consider on this issue.

1. Two-year colleges are vital to our nation, to the economy, and to the completion agenda itself. If you haven't yet read "The Good That Community Colleges Do," I would urge you to do so in order to gain a more detailed understanding of this point.

If more students are to complete college, we must first provide opportunities for them to enter college. Two-year institutions do just that, offering admission to students rejected by other, more-selective campuses. We serve any number of groups that are significantly underrepresented elsewhere: the academically underprepared, the economically underprivileged, minority students, and returning adults, just to name a few.

In most states, two-year colleges already get less money than other institutions. Further reducing that support will limit opportunities for thousands of students, which in turn will hurt our economy by reducing the number of educated workers. It will also negatively affect college completion—the very behavior that the threat of budget cuts was supposed to encourage.

2. It ought to be self-evident but apparently it isn't: Two-year colleges are different from four-year institutions. In fact, one of the most alarming things about the college-completion agenda, to me, is the way two- and four-year colleges are being lumped together, with similar outcomes expected of both. That makes no sense to anyone who understands higher education.

In most states, two-year colleges have very low admission requirements or virtually nonexistent ones known as "open-door policies." Their mission, in short, is to accept just about anybody. The vast majority of four-year colleges are at least moderately selective, admitting students based on test scores and high-school grades.

In addition, most students who enter a four-year college do so with the intent to stay and graduate. Many students at two-year colleges—perhaps the majority—have no such intention. They want to transfer as soon as possible, or maybe just pick up a course or two for certification or other reasons.

3. Two-year colleges are never going to have the same output as four-year colleges. Nationwide, graduation rates at two-year campuses hover in the range of 30 to 40 percent, while four-year institutions typically graduate 60 to 70 percent of their students.

Think about that for a moment. At a typical two-year college, about a third of the students have to take pre-college, "developmental" courses because they didn't have the skills to succeed in college when they arrived on our campus. It's not surprising that many of those students don't make it through to graduation; what ought to be surprising is how many of them do. Do we really want to close off higher education for those students by defunding their programs?

michaeljung/Shutterstock.com

Another third (or more) of students at two-year colleges have no intention of sticking around to graduate. Just the other day, I had the following conversation with a new student:

Student: How many hours do I need to transfer to Nearby State University?

Me: You probably need 24, at least, but 30 would be better. And it would be even better if you stayed here and got your associate degree. Then you'd have a degree to show for your efforts and NSU would be pretty much obligated to accept all your hours.

Student: How long would that take?

Me: Two years, if you go full time each semester or pick up some courses in the summer. You're looking at about 60 to 65 hours, depending on your program.

Student: (Long pause) Um, I think I just want to transfer as soon as I can.

I know, I know. I was supposed to say, "You vill graduate. Ve have vays to make you graduate." But who am I to make that decision for her? All I can do is provide accurate information, along with some decent advice, and let her make up her own mind. And if she transfers to Nearby State University after picking up 30 credit hours with us and then graduates, who's to say that we haven't played a vital role in her success?

4. Two-year colleges aren't all the same. Up to this point I've used "two-year colleges" as a blanket term, but within that category is a varied bunch of institutions with different missions. Some, like mine, are primarily "access institutions," portals into their state's university system. Others are more technically oriented, offering programs designed to funnel students into the workforce as quickly as possible.

And then there are what we call "comprehensive community colleges"—places where both functions (transfer and training) exist on the same campus, allowing students to move back and forth between both sides of the house. As I've argued before, this is America's uniquely egalitarian contribution to higher education. Instead of becoming stuck on a particular "track," students have the opportunity relatively late in the educational process to decide what they want to do with their lives.

In short, we can't lump all two-year colleges together any more than we can conflate two-year and four-year ones. We have to respect their varied missions and judge them ultimately on how well they fulfill those missions.

5. Two-year colleges have lots of special cases (and I don't mean athletes). After the meeting at which we were lectured for not graduating more students, a colleague who's working on her doctorate confided that she's the poster child for what's wrong with our college. "What do you mean?" I asked. She reminded me that, the previous year, she had taken a couple of courses on our campus to bone up for her Ph.D. language exam. But of course she had no intention of graduating from here. "So you see," she said, "I'm a failure."

Irony aside, situations like that are extremely common at two-year colleges. We have adults coming back to take courses for personal enrichment. We have transient students taking a math or English class over the summer. And we have loads and loads of dual-enrollment students, most of whom are just taking a course or two. This semester I'm teaching two early-morning sections of a course composed entirely of local high-school kids trying to pick up a few college credits before they go off to the University of Georgia or Georgia Tech next fall.

Is it to those students' advantage to complete some of their college coursework while still in high school? Obviously. By offering those courses, are we performing a service for them and the taxpayers of this state? No question. Then why should we as an institution be penalized because those students don't stay with us and graduate? Once again, that makes no sense.

So please, policy makers, don't throw the baby out with the bath water. Recognize that a one-size-fits-all standard does not work in higher education. Otherwise, we risk destroying the very system we're counting on to help us prepare students for life and work in the twenty-first century.

Discussion questions for "The Completion Conundrum":

1. What exactly is a conundrum, and what is the specific conundrum surrounding college completion?

    _____

    _____

    _____

    _____

    _____

    _____

    _____

    _____

2. In what ways do two-year colleges differ from four-year colleges?

    _____

    _____

    _____

    _____

    _____

    _____

    _____

    _____

3. In what ways do two-year colleges differ from each other?

_____

_____

_____

_____

_____

_____

_____

4. Why is it so important for policy makers to take those differences into account?

_____

_____

_____

_____

_____

_____

_____

42

Why Are So Many Students Still Failing Online?

Online learning has become the third rail in American higher-education politics: Step on it and you're toast.

That's especially true at two-year colleges and other access institutions, where many leaders have embraced online courses with an almost religious fervor. And we all know why. It's not because anyone is seriously arguing that online classes are consistently better than the face-to-face versions. And it's not even necessarily because students are clamoring for them (although they're clearly popular in certain segments of the population, such as stay-at-home parents, people with full-time jobs, and deployed members of the armed forces). It's because colleges can produce online courses much more cheaply while charging roughly the same tuition.

In other words, at many two-year colleges, online classes constitute the proverbial cash cow. And if you say anything about them—other than that we should offer more and more, forever and ever, virtual worlds without end, amen—then you will be branded as a heretic, ridiculed as a neo-Luddite, and shunned.

At least it sometimes seems that way. But isn't it time that we had an honest national conversation about online learning? With countless studies showing success rates in online courses of only 50 percent—as opposed to 70 to 75 percent for comparable face-to-face classes—isn't it time we asked ourselves some serious questions? Such as: Should every course be taught online? And should we allow every student—or any student who wishes to—to take online courses?

I sometimes joke with my first-year students, many of whom are seeking admission to our college's top-flight nursing program, that we used to offer an anatomy lab online until we started receiving complaints from people whose cats were missing. No doubt that joke is in poor taste, but it illustrates a point that seems to me self-evident: We can't teach everything online, nor should we try.

To all of you out there shaking your heads at my ignorance, can we perhaps find common ground? Can we agree that none of us would want to be operated on by surgeons who received all of their medical training online? If so, then perhaps we can agree that online learning has its limitations. The only debate is over where those limits lie.

That debate should be reserved for faculty members and academic administrators. The question is not whether online courses are more cost efficient (we already know that they are) or whether students like them. The only important question to ask about how particular courses and programs should be taught is, "What is in the best interests of students academically?"

I'll be the first to acknowledge that I don't always know the answer, and to admit that I've been wrong in the past. A few years ago, when we attempted to place an entire associate degree online, my college found itself struggling with a couple of courses in particular. One was our public-speaking course, which happened to be housed in the department that I chaired at the time.

Conventional wisdom back then dictated that you couldn't really teach a speech course online. To whom would the students give their speeches? How would they collectively become engaged as audiences or learn to analyze the speeches of others, as they do in a traditional classroom? I sided with the establishment. Speech, I decided, was just one of those courses that students would have to come to campus to take.

That is, until one of the faculty members in my department took it upon herself to solve the problem, through a combination of strategies that required students to videotape themselves; give speeches in front of church, school, or civic organizations; and observe and evaluate similar speeches by others. Her online public-speaking course became the template not just for our college but for the entire state system.

I still don't think an online speech course is quite as good as the face-to-face kind. It seems to me that there are distinct advantages to being in the same room with the professor and other students; that there are dynamics and experiences associated with the brick-and-mortar classroom that can't quite be duplicated via the Internet. But an online speech course can be almost as good. Done well, it could certainly provide students with the necessary knowledge, and teach them the requisite skills.

I think that's where we are with most online courses: They're not quite as good as face-to-face, but they're close enough. Are some of them just as good? No doubt. Might some be even better? Possibly. But a few, at least, should probably not be taught at all—"Advanced Brain Surgery" would be high on my list—and most are merely good enough.

For students who aren't able to attend college in the traditional way, "good enough" can be a godsend. But that doesn't mean that all students, or any student who wants to, should take online courses. Our collective failure to recognize that fundamental reality is primarily responsible for the high failure rates we see in online courses.

Years ago, when I was at another institution, and the online revolution was just gathering momentum, we were already noting that our online offerings had success rates that were much lower than in face-to-face sections. I recommended in a meeting of department heads that we consider instituting some sort of front-door controls. After all, we routinely test entering students to determine whether they're prepared for college-level math and writing courses; why not test them to see if they can handle online courses?

My suggestion was met with stony silence. Then the administrator running the meeting let me know, in no uncertain terms, that the college would never go for that idea, because it would limit online enrollment at a time when growth was needed for budget reasons.

In other words, "We don't care what happens to students at the end of the class. We just need them to sign up and stay on the roster long enough to count as enrolled." I never broached the topic again, nor to my knowledge did anyone else at that institution. I imagine many other professors made the same suggestion at other colleges, where it was similarly shot down.

But it's time to talk about it now. Online enrollments across the country are strong and growing, while success rates stay about the same: abysmal. I attended a session at the "Innovations 2011" conference a couple of months ago, held in San Diego by the League for Innovation in the Community College, where I learned that some colleges were beginning to experiment with the kinds of controls I recommended. Software companies now market products designed to determine, up front, whether students can handle the workload, the pedagogical approach (heavy on reading), and the technical demands of the online environment, and some of those products have shown promise. That sort of approach just makes a world of sense.

Unfortunately, many institutions still shy away from anything like that, because they're afraid of losing enrollment. Some are even complicit in perpetuating the notions that any student can succeed in online courses and that as many as possible should be encouraged to try. (I'm sure we've all seen multiple variations on the "Go to college in your PJs" marketing campaign.)

I'd like us to be more honest with students. Generally speaking, online courses are harder than face-to-face ones, not easier. Online courses require a tremendous amount of self-discipline and no small amount of academic ability and technical competence. They're probably not for everyone, and I think we need to acknowledge as much to students and to ourselves.

No one doubts that most courses will eventually have an online component, if they don't already. I have no problem with that. For the past couple of years, I've gradually been putting more and more of my course materials online. I agree with those who think that hybrid courses, incorporating face-to-face and electronic elements, are the future. Some concepts can be conveyed quite well online, while others really need to be taught in a traditional classroom.

In the meantime, though, we need to think long and hard about which courses should be taught fully online, and which students belong in online courses. If students and their prospective employers ever begin to suspect that, in our rush to offer everything online, we have oversold and underdelivered, then it's going to be too late for us to have that discussion. Politicians will have it for us.

Discussion questions for "Why Are So Many Students Still Failing Online?":

1. Should all college courses be offered online? Why or why not?

_____

_____

_____

_____

_____

_____

_____

_____

2. Should all students be able to take online courses? If so, why? If not, what criteria should students meet before being allowed to take classes online?

_____

_____

_____

_____

_____

_____

_____

_____

3. What steps can colleges take to raise success rates in online classes?

_____

_____

_____

_____

_____

_____

_____

4. What should students consider before signing up for online classes?

_____

_____

_____

_____

_____

_____

_____

43

Online Classes and College Completion

The latest buzzword in higher education is "completion." It combines the idea of enrollment growth with what we used to call "retention"—that is, getting more students into college and then keeping them there long enough to graduate or (in the case of community-college students) transfer successfully to four-year institutions.

The completion concept is nothing new. We've been focused on increasing enrollment since I started in this profession more than twenty-five years ago, and we've also spent countless hours talking about how to do a better job of retaining and graduating students. The results have been mixed, at best. According to the National Center for Education Statistics, college enrollment grew by 9 percent in the 1990s and a whopping 38 percent from 1999 to 2009.

And yet, as former Education Secretary Arne Duncan told PBS in a 2010 interview, completion rates have stagnated during those same two decades, with the United States slipping from first place to ninth among industrialized nations. "Other countries have passed us by," he said. "They're outworking us. They're outcompeting us." In other words, we've been doing a decent job of getting students in, but a poor job of getting them out with a degree in hand.

This time around, though, colleges may have added incentives to make retention a priority. President Obama has identified college completion as central to his economic agenda, calling education "the economic issue of our times" and vowing that America will once again "lead the world in college graduation rates by the end of this decade."

Moreover, governors and state education leaders have begun hinting strongly—and, in some cases, doing more than hinting—that future funds for colleges and universities may be tied to graduation rates rather than just to enrollment, as has traditionally been the case. As a result, community colleges and other access institutions, which are always looking to enlarge their slice of the pie and constantly fearful lest their already meager rations be further reduced, are rushing to get on board with the completion agenda.

I certainly agree that college completion is vital, both to our nation's economy and to our efforts to maintain an informed and engaged citizenry. Yet I'm concerned that some two-year institutions and systems might be taking the wrong approach, one that may ultimately prove counterproductive. Specifically (and predictably enough), many state systems have said that a key component of their plans to raise graduation rates involves increasing online offerings, despite strong evidence that online classes may have just the opposite effect.

For example, according to a report by the Bill & Melinda Gates Foundation, Washington state's Student Completion Initiative includes plans to "redesign ... high-enrollment-gatekeeper and precollege courses into online classes." A position paper on college completion produced by the National Conference of State Legislatures applauds Montana, among other states, for "expanding online learning options" and creating "a virtual community college as a low-cost option to expand access." And in my own home state, the Complete College Georgia plan calls for institutions to "increase the array of online programs ... to enable all students ... to effectively pursue college completion." Those are just a few examples of what appears to be a national trend.

At first glance, the idea seems to make a lot of sense: Surely if we make it easier for students to get the credits they need by offering as many classes as possible online, more will finish. And no doubt that approach is cost effective, at least in the short run. We can increase access without having to spend money upfront for infrastructure—money that, incidentally, we don't have. We can also reach potential student populations whose only access to college courses comes via the Internet.

Unfortunately, we seem to have forgotten that access and completion are not the same thing.

Simply getting more students to enroll isn't going to help much if too few of them ever finish. In fact, given Secretary Duncan's assertion that completion rates remain disappointing, even as enrollment grows, one might argue that we're setting many of those students up for failure.

To counter that argument, online enthusiasts point to a 2009 "meta-analysis" by the U.S. Department of Education that, they say, shows that online courses are not only cheaper and more convenient but also better. The report looked at ninety-nine individual studies of online learning conducted since 1996 and concluded that "on average, students in online learning conditions performed better than those receiving face-to-face instruction."

Nice try. But that study has serious flaws, especially as it pertains to community colleges. In the "Effectiveness of Fully Online Courses for College Students: Response to a Department of Education Meta-Analysis," Shanna Smith Jaggers and Thomas Bailey of the Community College Research Center at Columbia University point out that only twenty-eight of the ninety-nine studies examined in the Education Department report focused on courses that were fully online. Furthermore, only seven looked at semester-long courses, as opposed to short-term online programs on narrow topics, "such as how to use an Internet search engine."

In other words, out of all the studies reviewed by the Education Department, only a handful dealt with the kind of fully online, semester-long courses that are being touted as a means of increasing college-completion rates.

Even more alarming, for those of us on the front lines at community colleges, is the fact that all seven of those studies were conducted at midsize or large universities, five of which were rated as "selective" or "highly selective" by *U.S. News & World Report*. Those are not exactly the kinds of places that typically attract at-risk students—the ones least likely to complete their degrees. Community colleges do attract such students, and in large numbers.

Moreover, in six of the seven studies, withdrawal rates were not even mentioned, meaning that the research gauged only how well students performed after completing the course. The studies didn't tell us anything about those students who didn't complete the course.

Two other studies by researchers at Columbia's Community College Research Center do shed light on the role that online courses play in college completion—and the news isn't exactly good.

The more recent of the two, as reported by *The Chronicle* in July 2011, "followed the enrollment history of 51,000 community-college students in Washington state between 2004 and 2009 [and] found an eight percentage-point gap in completion rates between traditional and online courses." That comes on the heels of a 2010 study that reached similar conclusions about community-college students in Virginia: "Regardless of their initial level of preparation ... students were more likely to fail or withdraw from online courses than from face-to-face courses. In addition, students who took online coursework in early semesters were slightly less likely to return to school in subsequent semesters, and students who took a higher proportion of credits online were slightly less likely to attain an educational award or transfer to a four-year institution."

Did you catch that? According to the Columbia study, community-college students who take online courses are actually less likely to graduate or transfer.

© rawpixel.com/Shutterstock.com

Is it possible that we're taking the wrong approach?

Increasing access to college through more online offerings may indeed help with the first part of the completion equation: enrollment growth. But if, as the Columbia studies clearly show, the most at-risk students are less likely to finish when they "attend" classes online, then for that group of students this approach may actually do more harm than good.

That's precisely what Jaggers and Bailey conclude in their response to the Education Department's analysis:

> While advocates argue that online learning is a promising means to increase access to college and to improve student progression through higher-education programs, the Department of Education report does not present evidence that fully online delivery produces superior learning outcomes for typical college courses, particularly among low-income and academically underprepared students. Indeed some evidence beyond the meta-analysis suggests that, without additional supports, online learning may even undercut progression among low-income and academically underprepared students.

All of this reminds me of a television commercial I saw recently. I don't even remember what product or company was being advertised. I just remember that the gist was, "If you're tired of dealing with websites and automated phone systems, do business with us. We'll give you the personal touch. You can even talk to a live person." And I remember thinking, "Maybe this is the wave of the future. Maybe we've reached our saturation point with virtual communication, and the businesses that succeed in the next decade will be those that make you feel like a person interacting with another person rather than some disembodied collection of ones and zeroes."

If that's the case, then maybe this is one lesson that colleges—especially community colleges, the "people's colleges"—can learn from the corporate world. Perhaps what the most at-risk students really need, instead of being herded into online courses, is the "personal touch." Maybe they need more face-to-face interaction with instructors and other students; more conferences in their professors' offices; more private, one-on-one tutoring sessions; more hanging out with their peers in the student center between classes.

Maybe allowing those students to sit at home, alone in front of their computers, with little in the way of emotional support—not to mention, in many cases, educational support—is actually a bad idea. Maybe instead of doing everything we can to encourage them to take as many classes as possible online, we should be welcoming them to our campuses and into our classrooms.

If future funds for higher education really do follow completion rates, rather than just enrollment figures, then this approach could even end up being more cost effective for colleges in the long run.

Welcome to My Classroom: ESSAYS ON THE FIRST YEAR OF COLLEGE

Discussion questions for
"Online Classes and College Completion":

1. What exactly does "college completion" mean? Why is it so vital?

_____

_____

_____

_____

_____

_____

_____

_____

2. Why are so many states recommending offering more online classes in order to improve completion rates?

_____

_____

_____

_____

_____

_____

_____

_____

3. Is that strategy likely to have the desired effect? Why or why not?

_____

_____

_____

_____

_____

_____

_____

4. Can the help that low-performing students need be provided effectively in an online environment? Why or why not?

_____

_____

_____

_____

_____

_____

_____

The New Traditional Student

Over the past several years, as I've traveled around the country talking to graduate students about careers at America's two-year colleges and access institutions, I've had the pleasure of visiting some of the nation's most beautiful campuses.

I always avail myself of the opportunity, if I have time, to wander around, breathing in the atmosphere, taking in the sights and sounds. On a certain level, I identify with the students that I see hurrying to class or sprawled on the quad. I began my education at a selective private liberal-arts college, which, although small, had its share of well-manicured lawns, tree-lined walkways, and old stone buildings competing with aggressively modern brick architecture.

My memories of "going off to college" are probably very similar to theirs as well: loading up the family station wagon (today it would be a minivan or SUV), my parents helping me carry my stuff into the dorm, Mom making sure the bed boasted actual linens before hugging me goodbye.

And yet on another level, as a longtime professor and administrator at several different two-year colleges, I am increasingly aware that the nostalgic film playing in my head, as I walk those elite four-year campuses, is more akin to an old episode of *Leave It to Beaver* than to contemporary reality. My experiences and those of the students I encounter at elite campuses no longer resemble the common experience of many college students today. What we used to call "nontraditional" students—older, working, married, and maybe still living at home—now constitute a large and growing percentage of those attending college in the United States. In fact, they are fast becoming the new traditional.

Consider: The National Center for Education Statistics reports that of the 17.6 million people enrolled in college in the fall of 2011, only 15 percent were attending a four-year college and living on campus. Thirty-seven percent were enrolled part time, and 32 percent worked full time. Forty-three percent were attending a two-year college. More than a third were over age twenty-five, and a quarter were over age thirty. By 2019, the percentage of those over twenty-five is expected to increase by more than 20 percent.

Given the trends—which those of us who work at two-year schools have been observing for some time, and which are now playing at four-year campuses near you—how must faculty members adjust their thinking? And their teaching?

That's assuming, of course, that most faculty members want their students, regardless of age or circumstances, to persist and succeed. Because the National Center for Education Statistics has also found that nontraditional students are more than twice as likely as traditional ones to drop out in the first year.

Our colleagues in student services picked up on that trend long ago and began developing programs to help nontraditional students: assistance with financial-aid forms, special tutoring and counseling services, and new centers for veterans and for divorced women who were suddenly thrust into the role of breadwinner. Those are all wonderful programs, and much needed. And yet other research shows that one of the most important factors in determining whether nontraditional students succeed is their experience in the classroom—or what Sherry Miller Brown calls "academic integration." Brown, former director of the University of Pittsburgh's Mc-Carl Center for Nontraditional Student Success, said that if nontraditional students perceive their educational outcomes "to represent a fair exchange for time, effort, and money invested, they will be more committed to staying at that particular institution."

In other words, if nontraditional students are going to graduate, then much of the onus falls on classroom instructors. And since we seem to be finding more and more of those students on our rosters every year, perhaps we ought to start taking them into account as we design our courses, plan our lessons, and approach our teaching. Here are some suggestions.

Recognize special needs. Nontraditional students often have legitimate issues and concerns that differ from those of full-time students age eighteen to twenty-one. For example, many nontraditional students have been out of school for years, and are understandably anxious about returning. Every semester, it seems, I have a student come up to me after the first day of class—usually a woman in her thirties or forties—and say something like "I am so scared about your class. I haven't taken English in (fill in the blank) years."

I always try to allay her fears by explaining that writing is mostly about having something to say and that, because she's lived a little longer than some of the other students, she doubtless has more to say and will probably do very well. And it's true. Those students often end up being among the best in the class. But initially they don't know what to expect.

Nontraditional students also tend to have personal, family, and academic circumstances that are much different from those of younger students. Many are married with children (or unmarried with children). Many work long hours to support themselves and their families and to afford tuition and books—and still barely stay above water financially. In some cases, they might not have attended school for a decade or two. Their study skills may well have eroded. They may have forgotten much of what they learned. They may be unfamiliar with new technologies.

Design courses accordingly. The second step, then, is to take all of the above factors into account as you develop your syllabus.

For instance, rules aimed at keeping eighteen-year-olds from ditching class or dragging in late every day might not work for nontraditional students who have families, jobs, and lives apart from the college. They struggle with bus schedules, child-care issues, and constantly shifting demands at work. Penalizing them for being late or absent, the same way you might penalize a traditional student who stayed out drinking with his buddies or just slept in, doesn't strike me as either fair or productive.

Honestly, strict rules and harsh punishments will probably just drive nontraditional students away, leading them to conclude that college isn't for them. If accommodating nontraditionals means you have to change the rules for the entire class, then so be it. One day they will probably constitute the majority of your students, if they don't already.

You can help nontraditional students adjust academically by using frequent "refresher" sessions to reinforce basic skills. (I suspect those sessions might be just as valuable for your recent high-school graduates.) Don't hesitate to offer extra help in your office or refer people for tutoring.

You can also provide a measure of financial relief by placing course materials online, creating inexpensive course packs, or taking other steps to lower the cost of books and supplies. And once again, your traditional students will probably thank you, too.

© Monkey Business Images/Shutterstock.com

Demonstrate relevance. To keep nontraditional students engaged, emphasize as much as possible the connections between what they're doing in your class and what they'll be doing once they graduate. Remember what Brown said: Nontraditional students need to perceive "a fair exchange for time, effort, and money invested."

Try to regularly establish a clear link between course concepts and "real-world" outcomes. Show them how what they're learning might apply beyond the classroom, in their professional lives. Take every opportunity to incorporate materials from nonacademic sources, such as newspapers, magazines, and websites. Structure your assignments to mimic real-life work situations. You can even bring in a guest speaker from a local company or nonprofit group, perhaps someone who graduated from your program.

Roll out the welcome mat. Do whatever you can to make nontraditional students feel valued in your classroom. Remember, this experience may either be entirely new to them, or something they haven't done in years. Besides feeling anxious, they may feel conspicuous because of their age or the way they look, talk, and dress. Even if half of the class is over age thirty, all they see are the eighteen-year-olds in their skinny jeans and designer tops.

And yet these older students constitute a wonderful resource. They bring a wealth of wisdom and experience and even skills to the class, along with a perspective on life that may be very different, and infinitely more practical, than that of their eighteen-year-old classmates.

Take full advantage of those qualities. Do whatever you can to pull nontraditionals into class discussions, perhaps by introducing topics to which they can easily relate. If you can get past their inhibitions, and draw them out, you will find them to be a source of many entertaining and pertinent observations. Choose readings that might be relevant to their situations, and then structure writing and presentation assignments that encourage them to draw upon their experiences. Without showing favoritism, look for opportunities to praise their contributions.

Above all, take advantage of their wisdom and experience to create learning opportunities for young students. As someone who frequently uses editing groups in composition courses, one of my favorite strategies is to mix nontraditional and traditional students in one group. I find that the older ones tend to be quicker than their younger counterparts to identify problems with logic and detail, while students fresh out of high school can often help older classmates with arcane grammar rules and modern submission guidelines. It's a classic "win-win" situation: Everyone learns, and everyone benefits.

Or perhaps I should say "win-win-win," because traditional students aren't the only ones who will benefit from sharing the classroom with people whose life experiences are different from their own. You, as the instructor, will learn a great deal, too, becoming a better person and a better teacher for future generations of nontraditional-cum-traditional students.

Discussion questions for "The New Traditional Student":

1. What have the terms "traditional students" and "nontraditional students" historically referred to?

_____

_____

_____

_____

_____

_____

_____

_____

2. How are those definitions changing today?

_____

_____

_____

_____

_____

_____

_____

_____

3. How does the "college experience" of today's typical student differ from the experiences of previous generations?

_____

_____

_____

_____

_____

_____

_____

_____

4. What do nontraditional students bring to the classroom that instructors and other students should recognize?

_____

_____

_____

_____

_____

_____

_____

_____

Welcome to My Classroom: ESSAYS ON THE FIRST YEAR OF COLLEGE

Serving Our Dual-Enrollment Students

Lately, there's been a fair amount of debate at the national level over which program does a better job of preparing students for the rigors of college-level work—Advanced Placement or dual enrollment, in which high school students take college courses for college credit.

Whichever side you happen to be on, one thing is certain: Dual-enrollment programs remain popular at many community colleges and regional universities, and are likely to become even more popular as more parents realize the financial benefits of those programs. In most states, qualified high-school seniors (and, in some cases, juniors) can take college classes at little or no cost.

That means those of us who teach at institutions with dual-enrollment programs will continue to see an influx of high-school-age kids taking college courses. We would do well to consider their unique circumstances and special needs.

Personally, I've been involved with dual enrollment (or DE as it's known) in one way or another virtually my entire career. I've taught DE courses at local high schools, as well as special sections designated for those students at my college. In most of my regular courses, I've had plenty of high-school students mixed in with the usual students over age eighteen.

As department chair, I was largely responsible for scheduling and staffing dual-enrollment courses, as well as dealing with problems that arose in them. And when I was academic dean, our campus DE coordinator reported directly to me. I even went with him, on several occasions, to visit local high schools, talking to prospective students and schmoozing counselors and administrators.

I am also, as I mentioned in my blog post, a parent who has had three children taking advantage of dual enrollment. The first two took college classes full time during their senior years of high school, and each earned a full year of college credit—more than 30 semester hours. The third is taking some of his classes at the high school, but he will still finish with more than a semester's worth of college credit.

So I'm a big believer in dual enrollment, and I've had a great deal of experience with it. In fact, this semester I'm teaching a 7 a.m. course made up almost entirely of DE students, and I have at least a dozen more of them scattered throughout my other classes. So when I offer advice about serving such students, I do so as someone who has been there and done that, who has seen the potential problems and dealt with the fallout.

Here's what I recommend for faculty members teaching dual-enrollment students.

Treat them like college students. As I've explained elsewhere, a fundamental tenet of my teaching philosophy is that college students are adults; they should be treated and expected to behave as such.

But most dual-enrollment students are not, literally, adults. And they're certainly not used to being treated like adults at their high schools, where their days are extremely regimented, they constantly have someone looking over their shoulders, and they have to ask for a hall pass just to go to the restroom.

College, of course, isn't like that. Many DE students have told me that the biggest difference they find between high school and college is that, in college, they—not the teacher or the school—are primarily responsible for their own success or failure. Nearly all of them prefer it that way, but it takes some getting used to.

One of the best things we can do for dual-enrollment students, then, is to treat them as much as possible just like other college students, with the same expectations, freedoms, and responsibilities. Although some faculty members may hesitate to invest that much trust in seventeen-year-olds, my experience indicates that the vast majority will embrace their newfound "adulthood" and rise to the occasion, rather than taking advantage.

Treating your students like adults can be a challenge if your course meets on a high-school campus. You might not be able to allow them to leave the room to go to the bathroom or whatever. But as much as possible, I always try to treat my classroom like an extension of the college, regardless of where it's physically located. As I explain to students, my classroom is kind of like an embassy: As long as they're inside, they're in college.

Expect college-level work. Even well-prepared students—which the dually enrolled usually are—often need time to adjust academically to college.

Dual-enrollment students often find that, while their advanced high-school courses were demanding in terms of time and effort required, their college courses make different sorts of demands. Students are forced to learn new things, relearn old things in new contexts, and think in unfamiliar ways. Typically, college-level reading and writing require deeper analysis, more synthesis of ideas, and greater practical application. You're not doing DE students any favors if you water down the course curriculum to make it easier for them, or if you expect any less from them than from other students.

Again, it might be especially tempting to cut academic corners if your course is held on a high-school campus or is entirely made up of DE students. But if dual enrollment is to be a program that not only provides college credit but also prepares students for the rigors of upper-division coursework—that is, if DE courses are to be the literal equivalents of college courses—then we must use the same syllabi, the same assignments, the same grading standards, and the same learning outcomes.

But they do have special needs. All of that said, there are still some important differences between dual-enrollment students and regular college students.

Try as we might to treat them like adults, they are actually minors and, thus, far more reliant on, and accountable to, their parents or guardians than are adult college students.

I'm not suggesting that we violate FERPA guidelines with respect to DE students—personally, I treat them the same as other students when it comes to issues of privacy. But if a seventeen-year-old's parents decide to take him or her out of school for a family trip, for instance, that student has to go, and as instructors we need to be understanding and make allowances. (Of course, that sort of thing can happen with young college-age students, too, and I always try to be understanding about it. It's just that it's more common with minors.)

Many dual-enrollment students also tend to be active at their high schools. They play sports, cheer, serve on the student council, belong to clubs, and participate in drama productions and musical performances. Those are all important aspects of high-school life that I have no desire to deny students just because "they're in college now." But such activities do occasionally create some conflicts with their college courses.

When conflicts arise, I ask myself one question: If a regular college student had a similar conflict—if that student were going to miss a test because of playing in a ball game or attending a student-council retreat—would I hold it against the student? If the answer is no, then I make exactly the same allowance for a DE student.

Other problems emerge when a student's high-school calendar clashes with the college calendar—such as two different spring breaks. DE students attending classes on the college campus might not have any spring break: Their high school may be in session when the college is on spring break, and vice versa. That's when you might get parents taking the student out of school to go on a family trip. Such conflicts can usually be worked out at the administrative level, but individual instructors might still need to be flexible.

Personally, rather than taking a hard line in those situations, I've always found it more productive to bow to the inevitable, consider the needs of families, and allow students to make up any missed assignments while not holding such absences against them.

Remember that, in most cases, the college course these students are taking with you also counts as a high-school credit, which means that, if you're too much of a stickler, penalizing students for things that, as minors, they can't really control—or penalizing them for taking part in the very activities that count for so much on college applications—you might actually prevent them from graduating. In addition to the human toll such decisions can take, there's no quicker way to sink a dual-enrollment program than to earn that sort of reputation.

As much as possible, we need to treat DE students just like other college students while also acknowledging that, in some ways, they're not like other college students. If we're going to recruit and enroll them, we have to serve them appropriately, just as we seek to serve students with disabilities or students with military commitments. And that means recognizing their special needs and accommodating them where possible.

Discussion questions for "Serving Our Dual-Enrollment Students":

1. What's the difference between Advanced Placement courses and dual enrollment? Which is better for students? Why?

_____

_____

_____

_____

_____

_____

_____

2. What does it mean to treat students like adults? What ramifications does that approach have for dual-enrollment students in particular?

_____

_____

_____

_____

_____

_____

_____

3. What are some of the characteristics of dual-enrollment students that tend to make them exceptional college students?

_____

_____

_____

_____

_____

_____

_____

4. What are some of the special needs that dual-enrollment students might have, as opposed to traditional college students?

_____

_____

_____

_____

_____

_____

_____

Welcome to My Classroom: ESSAYS ON THE FIRST YEAR OF COLLEGE

Of Corporations, Corporatization, and Corporatism

In response to an article I wrote recently on the connection between corporate influence on higher education and the decline of shared governance, one reader wrote: "More 'corporations are bad' blather." Another congratulated me for "taking on the corporatization of higher education."

Both, unfortunately, missed the point. I wasn't trashing corporations. And I wasn't talking about corporatization; I was talking about corporatism.

Perhaps that sounds like a distinction without a difference. I would disagree. But before I go into that, let me first make it clear that I have no problem with corporations per se. I don't believe they're inherently evil. In my experience, corporations are as good or as bad as the people who run them. They have great potential for good—driving economic growth comes to mind—as well as great potential for bad. Just like most people I know.

It does seem that the larger a corporation grows—and the more the decision making and the responsibility for those decisions get spread around—the less socially responsible and accountable to the community it becomes. But that doesn't necessarily mean that even large corporations are inherently bad.

That said, for-profit corporations are not the same kind of entity as not-for-profit higher education institutions. The former are concerned primarily with making a profit, and only secondarily (if at all) with serving the public. The latter should be focused on the public good, first and foremost, and also on managing their resources wisely and being good stewards.

No doubt, in their efforts to be good stewards, there is much that colleges and universities can learn from responsible corporations about best practices in areas like accounting, purchasing, and financial management—areas in which many institutions are notoriously deficient. But when institutions start making decisions about academics and student services based solely on the bottom line, as if they were for-profit corporations, we refer to that as "corporatization."

And yes, I do believe that's a bad thing to the extent that it conflicts with our responsibility to serve the public. Corporatization is also antithetical to true shared governance, because the last thing bean-counters want is academics in a position to oppose the bottom-line agenda.

However, even worse than the corporatization of individual campuses is what I described in my last post as "corporatism." Corporatization is a set of practices, an approach to management. Corporatism is a larger philosophy which posits that all social institutions, including and perhaps especially public education, exist to serve corporations. In a corporatist society, the interests of the state become virtually inseparable from those of large corporations and their major-donor CEOs. We sometimes refer to this as "crony capitalism."

We already see this philosophy at work across the country in secondary schools, where the vast majority of students receive only the most basic instruction, which equips them for college only barely (if at all). Select students take more-advanced courses, and an even smaller number are placed into special programs that prepare them to be "the leaders of tomorrow." This closely mirrors the standard corporate structure in which most workers are basically drones, with a smaller management class and an even tinier cadre of executives.

The same philosophy is now finding its way into higher education. Corporate apologists and sympathetic politicians, with the support of large corporations and allied foundations, argue that higher education can function more efficiently by herding the vast majority of students—at community colleges, regional universities, and branch campuses—into massive "open" courses, vocational "training" programs with little or no academic component, and other quasi-educational venues. Meanwhile, the future leaders of our public and private sectors will continue to receive personalized instruction at their elite institutions.

That's the corporatist agenda, and it goes far beyond mere bottom-line decisions in the executive suite (although such decisions serve the corporatists well). It directly conflicts with our agenda as faculty members—or what ought to be our agenda, which is to provide the best possible education for all students, regardless of whether they're at Harvard or at a community college. That means teaching them to think for themselves, helping them reach their maximum potential as human beings, and preparing them not just for careers but for life. Corporatists, by and large, want only a limited number of people who can think for themselves. The rest should be able to perform certain specific job functions and otherwise do as they're told.

That's why corporatism and shared governance are natural enemies: because shared governance is the only means by which faculty members can fight back against corporatist attempts to subvert our ideals. And that's why the corporatists have recently ramped up their attacks on tenure and academic freedom—the twin pillars upon which true shared governance rests.

Discussion questions for "Of Corporations, Corporatization, and Corporatism":

1. What can colleges and universities learn from responsible corporations?

_____

_____

_____

_____

_____

_____

_____

_____

2. What is "corporatization," and how does it affect higher education?

_____

_____

_____

_____

_____

_____

_____

_____

3. What exactly is "corporatism"? How does it affect higher education?

_____

_____

_____

_____

_____

_____

_____

4. Do you think that corporatization and corporatism can co-exist with shared governance and academic freedom? Why or why not?

_____

_____

_____

_____

_____

_____

_____

Purging My Syllabus

Not wanting to sexually harass my students, much less be labeled a sexual harasser by the Department of Education, I have decided to review my Intro to Lit syllabus and remove any reading assignments that might contain offensive material.

Not that any reasonable person would find those reading selections offensive. But the DOE has apparently decided that the "reasonable person" test no longer applies, and that any "unwelcome speech" qualifies as harassment. Since my lit students seem to find nearly everything I say unwelcome, that's going to make teaching the course a little difficult.

Nor does it matter, apparently, that my purpose in the course is not to sexually harass anyone, or even necessarily to talk about sex. But the study of literature is the study of the human condition, of which sexuality is, regrettably, one aspect. Or at least it used to be, before the DOE ruled against it.

Accordingly, I am eliminating the following selections from my reading list, effective in the fall:

- Andrew Marvell's "To His Coy Mistress" and John Donne's "The Flea," two classic seduction poems. I've always thought my students rather enjoyed the vivid, earthy imagery in those works—and maybe learned something about metaphor in the process—but I now realize that they were merely feigning interest to mask their discomfort.

- "Hamlet," by William Shakespeare. As everyone knows, Shakespeare was a dirty old man, unless of course he was actually a woman. In Hamlet, the prince suspects that his mother and his uncle had an affair before conspiring to murder his father. That's not just adultery; it smacks of incest, for gosh sakes.

- "I Want a Wife," by Judy Syfers. In this classic feminist essay, Syfers says that she'd love to have a wife who is as responsive to her sexual needs as she is expected to be to her husband's. Such a frank discussion of female sexuality is bound to leave many in the class feeling harassed.

- "Wild Nights, Wild Nights!" by Emily Dickinson. Speaking of female sexuality, do we really want young people contemplating some nineteenth-century poet's love life, whether real or imaginary? Do we want them grappling with the imagery inherent in a line like "might I but moor tonight in thee"? The DOE apparently doesn't, and that's enough for me.

- "Hills Like White Elephants," by Ernest Hemingway. I almost left this story in, because it's a little hard to figure out at first what the two main characters are talking about. But once students understand that the young woman in the story is probably pregnant—out of wedlock, no less—and that the man is trying to persuade her to get an abortion, you can be sure that at least one person in the class will be offended.

- "Where Are You Going, Where Have You Been?" by Joyce Carol Oates. Ostensibly about fate versus free will or the nature of evil or some such nonsense, this short story actually deals with the apparent kidnapping, rape, and murder of a teenage girl. Even though the crimes themselves are not depicted in the narrative, it's pretty obvious what's going on. You can't get much more "unwelcome" than that.

As you can imagine, deleting those selections will pretty much gut my syllabus. I'll have to come up with some alternative readings if we're going to have anything at all to talk about in class. I don't know yet what I'm going to substitute, but I'm leaning toward "Winnie the Pooh," "Where the Red Fern Grows," and the Sears Roebuck catalog, Fall/Winter 1963.

We might even skip literature altogether—because, let's be honest, nearly all of it is potentially offensive—and just watch old episodes of *The Andy Griffith Show* online. Think of the rousing class discussions those will generate!

Then again, it might be better if we didn't have any class discussions at all. Who knows when somebody might say something unwelcome?

Discussion questions for "Purging My Syllabus":

1. Is it possible for professors to sexually harass their students by virtue of the readings they assign? If so, how? What would constitute harassment?

   _____

   _____

   _____

   _____

   _____

   _____

   _____

2. What do all the reading selections mentioned in this essay have in common?

   _____

   _____

   _____

   _____

   _____

   _____

   _____

3. Do students have a right not to be offended? Why or why not?

_____

_____

_____

_____

_____

_____

_____

4. What effect might the Department of Education's prohibition on "unwelcome speech" have on the college classroom?

_____

_____

_____

_____

_____

_____

_____

Straight Talk about "Adjunctification"

It's unclear precisely when the term "adjunctification" was born. It's mentioned as far back as 2000 in articles about the job market in the humanities. Linda Collins used the phrase in a speech in 2002 when she was president of the California Community Colleges' Academic Senate. Since then, the condition she so succinctly described—academe's overreliance on adjunct faculty members, especially at two-year colleges—has only gotten worse. More than half of all U.S. faculty members now hold part-time, contingent appointments.

That situation and what to do about it have become frequent topics of conversation in *The Chronicle* and elsewhere. Having followed the discussion closely, and having dealt directly with part-time faculty members for many years as a former department chair and academic dean (not to mention being a former part-timer myself), I've concluded that there is no single solution. Perhaps we can take steps to alleviate it over time, but only if we come to fully comprehend its various nuances.

Unfortunately, much of the rhetoric surrounding the hiring of contingent faculty members remains emotionally charged, which is understandable, perhaps, but not particularly helpful. Bitterness and frustration, however justifiable, lead to impractical demands, unrealistic expectations, and, in some cases, further inequities. As a counterpoint, I'd like to offer some dispassionate observations based on my thirty-plus years of experience in higher education.

Yes, an overreliance on part-time instructors harms the academic enterprise. It's no surprise that many studies have concluded as much, and I've seen the damage firsthand.

As the American Association of University Professors, among others, points out, the overuse of adjuncts harms students because it leaves them with fewer full-time professors who have the time—not to mention the office space—to meet with them one-on-one for advising, counseling, and tutoring. It harms adjunct faculty members themselves by creating a system in which they are poorly treated and even more poorly compensated. It harms full-time professors because there are fewer of them to take on committee assignments and other institutional responsibilities. It harms the faculty as a whole by diminishing the number of tenured professors with the freedom to speak out on issues of concern, and it harms the institution by undermining shared governance, which, in its true form, requires that a majority of faculty members possess such freedom.

Of course, everything I've just said is well known, and most readers would probably agree. What far fewer people might acknowledge, however, is that those talking points fail to tell the whole story. That's because the operative term in that last paragraph is "overuse"—which leads me to my next observation.

Some use of adjuncts is necessary. The idea that we can "fix" the "adjunct crisis" simply by turning all adjunct positions into full-time, tenure-track jobs is, frankly, unworkable. Most colleges need a certain number of adjunct faculty members in order to operate.

As a department chair, I argued every year for additional tenure-track lines. I saw that as part of my job, and a way to strengthen the department and better serve students. Once I became dean, however, I gained more insight into the overall instructional budget and quickly saw that we did not have the money to hire as many full-time faculty members as we would like. Often, the choice we faced was either to hire adjuncts or not offer certain courses at all.

It's easy to say states should just provide more funding so colleges don't have to make those tough choices. No argument here. But there's very little that faculty members can do individually, or even collectively, to change state funding formulas, other than vote and advocate for change. As a practical matter, state funding for higher education isn't likely to increase anytime soon, so colleges will continue having to balance the potential harm from the overuse of adjuncts against the harm that might result from not using them enough.

Adjuncting isn't always a bad thing. Constant focus on the negative aspects—low wages, lack of benefits, "free-way flyer" syndrome—has led many, I fear, to conclude that part-time teaching is itself a terrible evil. That's simply not true. Adjuncting has its advantages, even for those who hope one day to be on the tenure track.

For one thing, adjunct teaching provides jobs for thousands of people. Not the best jobs with the best pay, true, but paying jobs nonetheless. Do the math: If you have ninety sections in your department being staffed by thirty part-timers teaching three sections each, and you convert all those positions into full time, assuming a five-course load (as is the case at most two-year colleges), that means twelve people are out of a job. You might think it a kindness to put some of those people out of their misery, so to speak, but I doubt most of them would agree.

In addition, part-time teaching jobs constitute what passes for an entry-level position on many campuses, including community colleges and other access institutions. More and more of those schools are requiring job candidates for tenure-track positions to have the equivalent of two to three years of full-time teaching experience. How are most young academics going to get that kind of experience except by adjuncting? Some call that exploitation, and maybe it is. But if so, the problem is systemic and, like state funding formulas, unlikely to change. For now, teaching part time remains one of the best ways for people to get their feet in the door, at least at a two-year college.

And let's not forget that there are plenty of people who teach part time because they like it: stay-at-home parents who relish the intellectual stimulation of teaching a couple nights a week, local business executives and public officials who enjoy sharing their hard-earned expertise, retirees who always dreamed of teaching one day. Such people may constitute a minority of adjunct instructors, but their numbers are not insignificant.

Moreover, they bring a wealth of knowledge, experience, and enthusiasm to their work, and our campuses would be poorer without them.

Not everyone is tenure-track material. This is a hard truth, and I imagine my pointing it out here will not endear me to those who have been seeking tenure-track work for years without success. So let me be clear: I'm not saying people don't get tenure-track jobs because they don't deserve them. In addition to the fact that there are simply too many qualified candidates for too few jobs, the hiring process itself seems far too fraught with randomness and ambiguity to justify that kind of blanket statement.

I am saying, however, that some people should not make the cut. While it may be true, as many have argued, that academe is no longer a pure meritocracy (if indeed it ever was), merit still counts for something. And the standards for a tenure-track faculty member are, and should be, higher than those for a contingent faculty member because being on the tenure track involves more than just teaching and research. Before you put someone in a position in which he or she is likely to stay for thirty years, you must believe that person is sufficiently committed to the institution and the profession, will make a consistently positive contribution, and will be a good colleague.

One of the least logical assertions I've heard is that if a faculty member is good enough to be hired part time, he or she must be good enough for the tenure track. That's kind of like saying that just because someone is your friend, he or she would make a good roommate. We all know that isn't true.

As a former midlevel administrator and chair of many search committees, I've been involved in hiring quite a few of my college's adjunct instructors for tenure-track positions. In many cases, I knew them to be excellent teachers, and felt comfortable with the idea of them as permanent colleagues. But there have been other part-timers I recommended against promoting to the tenure track. As I saw it, my duty to hire good people for the institution outweighed any obligation I had to those people just because they taught part time on my campus.

New health-care regulations will undoubtedly alter the landscape. The Affordable Care Act's definitions of full time and part time, along with its requirements to provide insurance benefits accordingly, are bound to change the way that colleges and adjunct faculty members interact in the future. In fact, we're already starting to see that.

The most obvious change is that, at many colleges, part-time instructors are being assigned fewer sections, lest they reach the "full time" threshold stipulated by the government. Among those who support themselves solely or primarily by adjuncting, that will probably create more "freeway flyers"—academics who seek to cobble together a living by teaching part time at several institutions.

If long-term adjuncts are made to teach fewer courses, colleges may find themselves hiring more part-timers to cover sections. Or colleges could simply ask tenure-track faculty members to pick up the slack by teaching additional classes.

At first glance, none of the above strike me as positive developments. But I suppose the jury is still out. It would be great if the health-care act ends up motivating colleges to classify more faculty members as full time and offer them benefits, but that seems unlikely. It will be interesting to see what happens.

In the meantime, what can colleges do to counter the negative effects of adjunctification? For starters, I agree with Rebecca Schuman, who suggested in a recent *Chronicle Vitae* column that we should go out of our way to provide more opportunities for long-term adjuncts to compete for tenure-track positions.

I also believe colleges should lobby regional accreditation bodies to tighten restrictions on hiring part-time faculty. The industry standard has long been that no more than 40 percent of an institution's courses should be taught by part-timers. But in my experience, that's one guideline accreditors frequently ignore, and it seems too high to begin with. A better standard would be that adjuncts should make up no more than 40 percent of the faculty, teaching no more than 20 percent of a college's course offerings.

If those arguments fall on deaf ears at the accreditor level, then faculty members can always take them to the campus administrators, perhaps in the form of senate bills or faculty resolutions. Working together in good faith, with a shared concern for the welfare of students and the health of the college, we should be able to reduce the number of adjuncts over time.

But we're never going to get rid of them entirely, nor should we. In their own way, part-timers are as vital to the success of our campuses as tenured professors. And even if no one else recognizes that, we, as their colleagues, certainly should.

Reflection questions for "Straight Talk about Adjunctification":

1. What does the term "adjunctification" refer to?

_____

_____

_____

_____

_____

_____

_____

2. What are some of the negatives of a higher education system that relies heavily on adjuncts, or contingent labor?

_____

_____

_____

_____

_____

_____

_____

3. What are some of the positives?

_____

_____

_____

_____

_____

_____

_____

4. What effect might the Affordable Care Act and its potential successors have on the academic labor market?

_____

_____

_____

_____

_____

_____

_____

49

Why Not a Two-Tier System?

In recent years, some very smart people—like Michael Bérubé, Marc Bousquet, Anthony Grafton, and William Pannapacker, to name a few—have offered their thoughts, in *The Chronicle of Higher Education* and elsewhere, about how to fix graduate education and, by extension, the academic labor market—which, all seem to agree, has "unraveled" (as Bérubé put it).

I approach this issue from a different perspective: as someone who does not work at a prestigious research university but rather at a two-year teaching college; as someone with several decades of experience on faculty search committees; and as someone who does not hold a Ph.D. but instead something much closer to what Bérubé describes as "a rigorous four-year M.A."

Indeed, it was that passage from his *Chronicle* essay in February 2013, "The Humanities, Unraveled," that prompted me to enter this particular fray. Bérubé wrote: "Should there now be two doctoral tracks, one hard-core, old-school research with a traditional dissertation, and another more like a rigorous four-year M.A.?"

He then answered: "I think that is a solution few will want to pursue, because it opens onto yet another thorny issue, namely the fact that we have in effect already created such a two-tier system in the academic labor market, where we have a relatively small cadre of tenured faculty doing research and a much larger cohort of professors who are basically on a teaching track. It seems a mistake to institutionalize that division of labor still more emphatically by building it into the structure of doctoral education."

I have great respect for Professor Bérubé, but reading that passage left me wondering: Why not a two-tier system? Why shouldn't we at least consider it, given that nothing else seems to be working?

After all, as Bérubé acknowledges, we already have a two-tier system—it's just not a very satisfactory one for the people on the second tier, most of whom aren't there by choice. It's a system based not on rational criteria, such as qualifications, but on the whims of the labor market and, often, on luck. It's a system of haves (those who have permanent, relatively secure positions) and have-nots (those who don't, often regardless of their degrees and qualifications).

But what if we could create an equitable two-tier system? One that acknowledges the worthwhile contributions of those on both tiers? A system in which people on the second tier are there by choice, with an opportunity to earn a decent living in their profession? There is interest: An October 14, 2012, article in *The Chronicle* on the notion of two tracks for faculty members attracted dozens of comments.

Such a system might well offer solutions to the two main problems with the academic labor market: namely, the glut of Ph.D.s and the resulting "underclass" of highly qualified people who might never find secure, permanent employment in their fields.

A pipe dream? Perhaps, but it's one worth exploring. Instituting a system like the one I'm about to describe would require major changes on the part of both graduate programs and hiring institutions.

But first, for those who remain skeptical (if not hostile), can we acknowledge that other professions have employed two-tier systems for a long time, quite successfully? People who don't have the time, money, patience, or desire to go to law school can pursue rewarding and relatively high-paying careers as paralegals. They might still decide to go to law school some day, and in fact would probably enjoy a distinct advantage, but in the meantime, their paralegal work is a respected and valued career path in its own right.

Perhaps a closer parallel to what I'm proposing can be found in the medical profession. As health-care costs have exploded in recent years, the industry has adapted by creating more and more "second-tier" positions for physician assistants and nurse practitioners. These are highly educated, well-respected (and, in many cases, well-paid) medical professionals who are being entrusted with tasks once reserved for doctors.

More to the point, they aren't people who couldn't find jobs as doctors, nor are they necessarily people who wanted to be doctors but somehow "fell short." They are professionals who made a conscious, rational choice and opted into the second tier of medicine.

Inherent to this two-tier system is the implicit understanding that people don't always need to see a doctor. I undergo a checkup every few months in order to keep my hereditary high-blood pressure under control, and I've probably seen my doctor twice in five years. Meanwhile, I've established an excellent relationship with the office's physician assistant, who has shown herself fully competent to treat my condition.

Perhaps we in higher education can learn from that model. Is it absolutely necessary for every college student, in every class, to sit at the feet of a Ph.D. professor? Community colleges have demonstrated that it's not, and most universities have implicitly agreed by relying heavily on graduate students to teach lower-division courses. So if it's not essential for college students to be taught by Ph.D.s, then why are we still producing so many Ph.D.s?

Here's my proposal: Graduate schools should create a degree that specifically qualifies recipients to teach in college but not necessarily to be researchers. This new hybrid degree would bring a lower salary than a doctorate, but would take far less time and money to earn than a doctorate. A college-teaching degree would carry more weight and respect than a master's, which, as many critics have noted, has become somewhat watered-down in recent years (if not in the sense that the degree itself has become less rigorous, then at least in the sense that more and more people seem to have one).

Our colleagues in elementary and secondary education have long had an alternative degree in their profession—the "education specialist" degree, or Ed.S., which is basically a master's plus 30 semester hours. Academe could adopt a similar model, perhaps even calling it a "specialist's degree" in college teaching. To earn that degree, students would have to complete 30 or so additional credit hours, including courses in pedagogy, beyond what would normally be required for a master's. Then they could finish with some sort of teaching-focused capstone project or thesis (but not a dissertation).

To make such a degree practical and attractive to students, departments would need to take several steps, beginning with making it much harder to get into a Ph.D. program than it is now. Only those students with demonstrated potential to become first-class researchers—and with a burning desire to do so—would be accepted. The faculty would have to determine what constitutes "demonstrated potential to become a first-class researcher," but, clearly, many of the people admitted to Ph.D. programs these days would not qualify. Such a step would, in time, go a long way toward alleviating the oversupply of Ph.D.s.

At the same time, no graduate professors would need to lose their jobs. Departments would be creating a second track, the specialist track, and those students would take many of the same courses as their Ph.D.-seeking classmates. If the specialist track did, in fact, become a realistic route to gainful employment, some departments might even see an influx of students.

Along with creating distinct degree programs for teachers and scholars, departments would also need to create two tracks to support graduate students: teaching assistantships for those in the specialist program, and research-only assistantships for those in the Ph.D. track. Departments that have relied heavily on doctoral students to teach entry-level courses could transform those many T.A. positions into a smaller but still sizable number of full-time posts filled by candidates with specialist degrees in college teaching.

Of course, it's not just the graduate departments that would need to change the way they do business. For an equitable two-tier system to work in academe, the end users—colleges and universities that hire faculty members—would have to make significant concessions, as well. For one thing, institutions would need to recognize the specialist degree as a valid qualification for teaching the vast majority of the courses—all, perhaps, except for a handful of upper-division and graduate-level courses.

Second, institutions would need to make a commitment to hiring more full-time instructors and using fewer adjuncts. But the idea is that, because they wouldn't be paying teaching specialists as much as they pay research Ph.D.s (just as physician assistants don't earn as much as doctors), institutions would find that they are able to finance more full-time faculty positions.

In particular, colleges with teaching missions—two-year and small liberal-arts institutions—would need to hire more candidates with the teaching degree and correspondingly fewer Ph.D.s. That would potentially create a lot of additional full-time positions, given that salaries would be lower for teaching professionals than for scholars.

If nothing else, graduates of teaching-specialist programs wouldn't be in school for a decade and so wouldn't incur as much debt. And they would earn a credential that could well qualify them for other jobs, such as teaching at secondary schools.

I understand that many readers will think this is a harebrained notion, and perhaps it is. Others may conclude that the idea is simply impractical. But what we're doing now isn't working and hasn't worked for some time. Minor tinkering with the system, tweaking it here and there, doesn't seem to be helping much, either. It's time to blow up the system and put something else in its place—something that takes into account current realities and offers more hope for people entering our profession.

Reflection questions for "Why Not a Two-Tier System?":

1. What is the essential problem with the current academic labor market?

_____

_____

_____

_____

_____

_____

_____

_____

2. How have other professions reacted to perceived inequities in their labor markets? How has that worked?

_____

_____

_____

_____

_____

_____

_____

_____

3. What are some objections to a two-tier system? Are they valid? Why or why not?

_____

_____

_____

_____

_____

_____

_____

4. What problems might such a system alleviate? What problems might it create?

_____

_____

_____

_____

_____

_____

_____

We Have to Protect Ourselves

If you're a college faculty member, or a prospective faculty member, do yourself a favor: Google the phrase "professor under fire." Many if not most of the thousands of hits have something to do with social media—in particular, with Twitter, Facebook, YouTube, or blogging. Social media constitutes the classic Catch-22 for academics: We can't ignore it or avoid it, nor do most of us want to, yet it gets us into more trouble than anything else.

As born pedants and guides, we find the opportunity to reach new audiences and interact with people, including students, irresistible. But there are times when we should resist that impulse. And there are other times when, even if we don't put our words out there for public consumption, there's a fair chance one of our students will do it for us.

A series of recent incidents involving professors and social media has focused our attention on the politically fraught nature of that relationship. Or at least it should have. Instead, each new episode seems to catch us by surprise, leaving us more troubled and outraged. We appear to have adopted the stance that social "media" is just that—merely an alternative medium—and our words are no different whether spoken in a faculty meeting or tweeted online. We assume the great institutions that have historically afforded us protection on campus—tenure and academic freedom—will likewise protect us when we venture outside the academy onto websites and blogs.

That has turned out not to be true in several high-profile cases. Professors have been censured, suspended, and even fired for things they have tweeted, blogged, or posted on Facebook—or things they said that other people have posted. (Feel free to Google "professor under fire" to read about some of these cases. I decided to write this without mentioning any names because I don't want to further embarrass anyone, pick at any scabbed-over wounds, or add to the number of search-engine hits.)

When we do step outside our roles as faculty members, aren't we protected by the First Amendment, just like any other citizens? Perhaps. But of course even First Amendment protections have limits. And in the case of "public employees," which most faculty members are, the landmark Supreme Court ruling in *Garcetti v. Ceballos* certainly blurred the lines between public and private speech. When are we speaking (or tweeting, or posting) "pursuant to our duties," and when are we speaking as private citizens? The legal profession is still debating that one.

The upshot is that, as professors, we can no longer rely on tenure, academic freedom, or even the First Amendment to protect us when we "speak." We have to protect ourselves. Here are some suggestions for doing just that.

Watch what you say—and how and where you say it. You would think such commonsense advice would hardly need to be repeated for adults with advanced degrees. But apparently it does. Most of the hot water that professors find themselves in, with regard to the Internet, results from their saying the wrong thing in the wrong forum, or saying the right thing in the wrong way.

Let's start with the classroom. Perhaps the simplest thing you can do to stay out of trouble is to teach your subject without injecting politics into class discussions where it has no relevance. If political issues are relevant to a particular discussion, then make sure students understand how. Try to discuss politics as dispassionately as possible so students recognize that you're not simply trying to indoctrinate them into a particular point of view. Otherwise, you may find yourself starring in the latest viral YouTube video.

And when it comes to sharing your views on social media, ask yourself one simple question: Are you intentionally phrasing your post to create a stir, or are you seeking to be understood without giving undue offense? That's especially important on sites like Twitter, where you have so little space to work with. The bottom line: If you're trying to stir things up, you probably will—and you might not enjoy the aftermath.

© Infinite_Eye/Shutterstock.com

Draw clear boundaries between "official" and "personal." A few years ago, the previous administration at my college instituted a couple of policies that seemed designed to discourage people from speaking out publicly on controversial educational issues. One of those policies listed the potentially dire consequences for those who "represented the college" without authorization. (I have since heard of other colleges and universities instituting similar policies.)

My first response was to begin separating, as much as possible, my work as a state employee from what I have come to consider my personal work. That proved challenging because much of what I write as a "private citizen" has to do with my experiences in academe. However, I chose to draw the line in a very specific place: Henceforth, any activity not directly connected to my official job description I would treat as personal, not "work related."

That's why I don't list most of my blog posts or online editorials as "publications" on my annual report to my employer. Doing so, I believe, would move those activities into the realm of "pursuant to my duties" and give the college a degree of control over them that I don't want it to have. Also, I rarely mention my college by name, and, in situations where acknowledgment of my affiliation is unavoidable (as in *The Chronicle,* for instance, where writers must list their title and institution), I have asked the editors to add a disclaimer like the one you see at the bottom of this column.

And of course I don't make any reference to my employer on my Facebook page (which is purely personal, in any case) or on either of my Twitter accounts (one personal, one professional).

Sure, it's possible for an institution to punish you for things you write or post as a private citizen, but you're only making it easier if the administration can show that you were speaking as a "representative of the college." Sadly, when colleges and universities play that game, they are the ones that lose out in the long run. They sacrifice a great deal of positive publicity (since most of what professors would say would actually reflect well on their employers) in hopes of avoiding the rare scandal.

But that's their problem. I'm just concerned with keeping myself out of the administration's cross-hairs—even though we now have a new administration that seems friendlier to faculty members with a public persona. Those policies I mentioned are still on the books, if somewhat modified, and I don't want to give a future administration any ammunition.

Use your own equipment—and time. My second reaction, when those campus policies were first introduced, was to go out and buy my own laptop computer. Along with the policies came a verbal reminder, during a faculty meeting, that the college owns our computers and can go through our hard drives and email anytime it so desires. I didn't think that would actually happen, but I wasn't taking any chances.

Up to that point, I had used my college-issued laptop for practically everything, including blogging, posting on Facebook, and so forth. Now I reserve it solely for activities that are directly related to my job as a professor, such as communicating with students, colleagues, and supervisors by email, maintaining the website for my classes, and submitting various forms and reports. For everything else, I use my personal computer.

Not only do I avoid using my college-issued machine for "personal" activities, I don't even use the college's server. Although I often carry my personal laptop to work and use it for "official business," because that can be easier than switching back and forth between machines, I make it a point not to post on Facebook or Twitter and not to submit a blog post or column from the office. I also have a private email address that I use for all of my noncollege work when I'm away from the office.

In addition, I do almost all of my public writing on my own time—that is, not during office hours or in between classes. I know a professor's job is such that "on the clock" has little meaning. (For instance, I do most of my grading at home, after regular working hours, like most faculty members I know.) But once again, I'm trying to draw a clear line between my college work and my own work.

Organize, advocate, and resist. Perhaps my advice here strikes you as a bit paranoid? If so, then either you don't have a public persona or else you haven't faced the kind of challenges that I've had, which is not to say you won't. Indeed, if this column has a theme, it's that perhaps we should all be a little more paranoid.

But that doesn't mean all is lost. Those two policies I mentioned have been "somewhat modified." That's because after they were first introduced, a small group of faculty members (including yours truly) organized a protest: We informed our colleagues of the policy's dangers by email, we lobbied administrators, and we pressured members of the faculty senate. Ultimately, the policies were watered down to the point where we could live with them—barely.

Of course, the problem isn't just local. It's national, as your Google search will show. If institutional policies that restrict faculty speech concern you, then you should join or support a national organization that fights for faculty rights, such as the American Association of University Professors or the Foundation for Individual Rights in Education. And you can always be active on your own campus, serving as a policy watchdog and joining with like-minded colleagues to advocate for faculty rights.

My own situation has improved greatly over the last eighteen months. No one in the current administration (as far as I know) has gotten upset about anything I've posted in that time. But I'm still writing this at home, late in the evening, using my own laptop.

Reflection questions for "We Have to Protect Ourselves":

1. How are college faculty members getting themselves in trouble on social media?

_____

_____

_____

_____

_____

_____

_____

2. What is the attraction of social media for faculty members? What are its drawbacks?

_____

_____

_____

_____

_____

_____

_____

3. Does where you say it and how, matter as much as what you say? Explain.

_____

_____

_____

_____

_____

_____

_____

4. What are some steps faculty members can take to protect themselves on social media and elsewhere?

_____

_____

_____

_____

_____

_____

_____

Welcome to My Classroom: ESSAYS ON THE FIRST YEAR OF COLLEGE

CPSIA information can be obtained
at www.ICGtesting.com
Printed in the USA
LVHW02s1150180318
569648LV00006B/8/P